Our Trees

By buying this book you also bought the
right to get a tree planted.

Go to **www.pinetribe.com/planting**
to claim your tree.

Going digital is good for the reader, good for the author and good
for the planet. That's why at Pine Tribe we only deliver digital books and print-
on-demand to minimise waste. But that's just the start of our quest. We plant
lots of trees. We just love trees. Maybe you do too.

DON'T DESPAIR

Letters to a modern man

Don't Despair - Letters to a Modern Man
© Matias Dalsgaard & Pine Tribe Ltd. 2014

Translator: Patrick Stokes *www.patrickstokes.com*
Editors: Julia Hilliard and Kalimaya Krabbe
Cover design: Patricia Hepe
1. edition 2014

ISBN: 978-0-9912609-4-2

www.pinetribe.com/matias

Pine Tribe Ltd.
International House
1 St Katharine's Way
London, E1W 1UN

DO ALL THINGS WITHOUT
MURMURINGS AND DISPUTINGS:
THAT YE MAY BE BLAMELESS
AND HARMLESS.

- ST. PAUL

PREFACE

Dear reader,

Last winter, I received a series of letters, which I have decided to publish here. They are personal letters. They are written to me, and are about me. The letters have helped me to achieve a more authentic understanding of myself, and they gave me renewed courage to live during a difficult period. I'm convinced that others will also get something out of these letters. For even though the letters are about me, they are just as much about the universal human question: how can I find myself and become happy?

The letters are written by my maternal uncle, Morten. He and I have always had a rather unusual relationship. On the one hand, being family, we have always been very close to each other. In many ways he is my closest family. On the other hand we've never fully understood each other. Morten is a priest, and his life in the church has never really held much interest for me.

I'm an economist, and my life in the world of money has no doubt always bewildered or even repulsed Morten. I doubt that we will ever really understand each other. But the letters have shown me that perhaps Morten understands me, and the things that drive me in life, better than I'd thought.

This correspondence came about against a very unhappy backdrop, some months before, my wife Agneta had left me. One night I came home from work and she was gone, along with our one-year-old son. Without warning. The life I had been leading up to that point suddenly fell apart. Agneta had left behind a short message. I remember wondering at first why they weren't home; shortly after that, a piece of paper on the kitchen table caught my eye. I took the paper in my hand and recognised Agneta's handwriting. "Rasmus, listen carefully now…" it started. As my eyes scrolled through the lines on the paper I felt a silent, monstrous panic rising like icy water all around me. I had not seen it coming, and I had no idea what I should do.

Actually, when I say that I hadn't seen it coming, that's not entirely true. The truth is I hadn't *wanted* to see it coming. I had already been on the way down a very steep slope, and Agneta had tried many times to tell me that our life together had become intolerable. She tried to make me see that I was about to drag us both down together – but I hadn't listened. So in fact, her leaving me was far from without warning.

I suddenly found myself in a hole I could not drag myself out of. My memory of the period that followed is actually somewhat hazy. I don't remember exactly what I did or thought about, only that everything seemed to be falling down on top of me, and that I was completely adrift. For a time I tried to prop myself up with work, but it offered only a brief respite. After struggling in vain for some weeks I was put on sick leave.

Like the rest of the family, Morten had been there for me and had helped as best he could. But the only thing I had any use for at first was peace and quiet, and so there was a limit to how much others could help me. But after a while I gradually began to recover. Having been disoriented and unable to rouse myself at first, I now tentatively began trying to get my bearings in the world again. I began to consider my situation and what it would take to start living again – and to be able to keep going.

And so one day I asked Morten for advice. As I said, in many ways Morten has been the family member closest to me, and so it was natural for me to ask for his advice. I certainly could not have foreseen that his advice would end up consisting of the following series of letters. Nor were the letters the result of any grand plan on his part. But they turned out to fit the situation well. In any case: I asked for his help, and this is what I got.

I have only half-understood – if that – much of what is in the letters. But I've understood as much as I could, and have taken on board what I found useful. My hope is that others will be able to do the same. Maybe someone else will be able to get even more out of the letters than I have. That's why I have chosen to put these letters out there – even though in doing so I put more of myself on show than I normally would.

Morten was opposed to publishing the letters at first. He just didn't think that they lent themselves to publication. After I made several attempts to convince him he finally gave in, but only on the condition that he would have nothing to do with the publication. That's why I ended up editing this book – so allow me to make a couple of comments about how I've gone about it.

The letters appear in the order in which I received them. As the letters were written over a long period of time, we naturally saw and spoke to each other many times during the process. Sometimes I even wrote an answer or sent some questions back to Morten. Nonetheless I have chosen not to publish my own reactions and replies. They don't have the same universal character as Morten's letters, and so you don't need to associate his letters with my more or less random, personal thoughts. At the same time, there are certain places where I cut sections out that either seemed needlessly repetitive, or were particularly private in nature. Also, in order to avoid exposing individuals or organisations unnecessarily, I have removed or obscured some names in the text.

The letters fall into two sections. The first is analytic and critical in character, while the second is more instructive and positive. Morten must have meant for his correspondence to fall into two parts like this. However, it isn't a hard and fast distinction. In addition, and in spite of all my attempts to clean it up, there are no doubt a number of repetitive and superfluous sentences along the way. But I doubt that a more thorough attempt to make the book's composition clearer would have helped. The topic – which is me, or you! – is after all something which, when all is said and done, has neither a clear beginning nor a clear ending. So a little bit of repetition won't hurt. In any case, in my own reading,

I for one have found pleasure in some of the letter's repetitions and variations on the same theme.

I have chosen the book's title and subtitle, as well as the chapter titles. The quote from Paul which I have placed at the start of the book came with one of the letters. I would really have liked to use words like "self-development" or "personal growth" in the title. But as a small gesture to Morten, I won't. I've often heard him speak with contempt about modern notions of self-help or personal development. It seemed to me that his initial reluctance to publish the letters was partly out of fear of becoming a "self-help author." That just isn't his style.

However, I believe, and hope, that these letters will be a kind of self-help aid for you. Naturally, I can't know if that will be the case. But here you have the letters – and the chance to see for yourself. Enjoy the reading.

Best,
Rasmus Dam
Copenhagen, March 2014

CONTENTS

PREFACE   7

INTRODUCTION   14

PART 1

THE WAY YOU LIVE   23

YOUR STORY   41

A Narrative Period   41
A Psychological Period   51
A Spiritual Period   61
A Narrative Period, Once Again   74

VARIOUS CONDITIONS   79

Self-absorption   79
Worry   87
Exceptionality   91
Individualism Without Personality   95

PART 2

BEING YOU   101

DON'T DESPAIR   115

FORMS OF NON-DESPAIR   129

    Joy   132
    Courage   136
    Grief   140
    Humility   144
    Humour   148

LIFE ON EARTH   153

YOU WITHOUT GOD   169

CONCLUSION   175

INTRODUCTION

Dear Rasmus,

I have been thinking about the questions you asked me yesterday, thinking about our conversation. And the more I thought about it, the more it became clear to me that the things I said were not really the things I wanted to say. Perhaps it was because we had so little time, or perhaps I needed to think about the matter some more. But it could also be because the things I actually have to say are so different from what you initially asked about, that the rather rushed form of the conversation unavoidably led to misunderstandings. I think it's the latter. So I am writing to you. I hope that in writing this down I can work out and say some of those things which didn't seem like they could be said in our conversation.

It was a dreadful shock to me when Agneta and Alexander left you, and then to see your reaction. Now, there is nothing particularly remarkable about the fact that you fell apart and lost your bearings in such a violent way. As I've said many times, in my view that was a perfectly natural reaction. What's more surprising is that you are already in such high spirits that you've started to consider your life and your future again. I thought it would have taken more time before life and the future once again had the pleasure of your company, so to speak. It pleases me greatly to see that you're recovering. But I don't want to push you into thinking about things which can wait for now. The most important thing is that you give yourself the time you need.

But if you feel you are ready for some more fundamental reflection on yourself and your life, and if you would like to hear my views on these matters, then I'd be happy to offer them.

Although I don't think I said what I really wanted to say when we spoke yesterday, that doesn't mean what I said was wrong. As best I recall, what I said was, in itself, perfectly fine. The problem is that you didn't seem to hear what I said. You seemed *unable* to hear what I said. Even though we know each other about as well as people can know each other, our understandings of life and of what it is to be a person are vastly different. We speak the same language and it seems as if we understand each other well enough, but the words have one meaning for me and another for you. You would like my advice on how you can best get ahead in life, and I would like to help. But the life I would like to help you with is different to the one which you asked me about. And so you listened to my advice without really hearing it.

Now it is far from clear that I am the right person to ask for help about how to get ahead in life. I've had my share of defeats, and I certainly didn't always just pick myself up and move on with my head held high. But I have never been struck down with periods of total disintegration and disorientation like you have. Something has always held me together, and maybe I really do have something to teach you about what that is. When I haven't broken down in the same way you did, that is certainly not because life has, in an outward sense, been easier on me than it has on you. If anything, it's been the other way around. And it's certainly not because I'm stronger than you either; I doubt that anyone is. Instead, what has helped me get through has been a very different sort of self-understanding to the one you seem to live by. So if I do have something to teach you, it will be on the level of understanding yourself.

In that respect, your breakdown is not, in itself, your real problem. As I said, it seemed to me entirely natural, and it would have been more worrying if you had carried on unaffected, as if nothing had happened. It was a misfortune that Agneta left, and it was a misfortune that you lost your footing in such a dramatic way. But as I see it, and as I tried to say yesterday, the problem goes deeper than that. The disintegration that you experienced is, to my mind, a reflection of a far more fundamental disintegration which has been lurking beneath the surface this whole time. I was sorry to see how this hit you, but – to be honest – I wasn't surprised. I've always had the sense that at some point the chaos within might break loose. It has always seemed to be just a matter of time, and then Agneta became the thing that finally popped the cork out of the bottle.

So if I am to contribute to your improvement, you will need to let me speak on the proper level. I don't have much practical advice to give you. I can't tell you how you can quickly land another job, or how you can quickly win Agneta back. I can hope and pray that this happens, but I am no sage for that kind of advice. What I can speak about, however, is the chaos and disintegration that seems to reign within you on a very fundamental level. I can speak about how your self-understanding – or lack thereof – drives you to the brink of collapse. If you will listen to me, then, it could be that there is something for you to learn. But what there will be to learn will be something different from what you first asked about.

If you listen to what I have to say, it will require you to set aside, for a time, your most immediate wishes and questions and allow yourself to hear something that might, in the end, mean your wishes and questions must change.

∗∗∗

There are different paths we could take into a discussion of what I take to be the real challenge you face. No single path is necessarily the right way, but I will start by talking about one of the subjects which came up several times in our conversation yesterday: happiness. You said several times that you hoped to get back to living your life and taking pleasure in the things that you once could. I would be very happy to see you get back to living life and finding happiness in it again. Except I doubt that "again" is the right word, because I don't think that you truly found pleasure in life before your breakdown either. I tried to say that yesterday, too, but what I really wanted to say didn't come across clearly.

Even before Alexander came into the picture, and the storm clouds seriously began building up to your current crisis, I saw with concern that you were living a life which seemed to be devoid of happiness. Something about you constantly seemed to be standing in the way of you really being able to find happiness in life. Rather than helping you win back a happiness that perhaps was never there in the first place, I'd therefore like to talk to you about the more fundamental absence of happiness in your life up to now, and of how this absence seems to be connected to what I'm calling your self-understanding.

✳ ✳ ✳

You are now 34 years old. You have already achieved much in life. Your clever head has carried you through life at a pace which most people would envy. In these last few years in the Finance Ministry you have once again outdone yourself, and have advanced through the system faster than anyone your age has before. Your achievements have never surprised me or others; if anything, your success was entirely expected. Even when you were quite little, you created expectations, great expectations, among all of us who were watching you. And you never had trouble living up to those expectations. In the first years of your childhood I didn't see quite as much of you as I would have liked. These were your parents' 'political years.' As we've talked about before, around that time your mother and I had even more trouble than usual understanding each other, and we both decided that these misunderstandings would be least painful if we refrained from seeing each other. But after the divorce your mother needed my help, and as Lene and Margrethe were getting bigger by that stage, another child was more than welcome in our home. They loved your visits, and I certainly didn't mind having a little male company in the family either. We have been as close as any family could be ever since. I will spare you the attempt to express how much having you in my life has meant to me. I think – I hope – that you are clear about that – even, or especially, if the things that I'll try to say to you here seem rather blunt or pitiless.

When I think back to my time with you as a child, it seems that the absence of happiness which I sense in you today was already beginning to develop. Or – how shall I put this – your capacity for happiness was already shutting down. For other children it seemed natural to lose themselves in play, yet there was always something reticent about you, something half-hearted about the way you played. It seemed as if you always secretly had one eye fixed backwards while you moved forwards. I noticed this many times, but hoped that the anxiety or nervousness of which it must have been a symptom would go away of its own accord with age. I hoped that at some point you would begin to show the world the confidence which came more naturally to other children. Being an intelligent child has never been easy. Childhood is not suited of thinking too much, and a bright head must often spend some of its adult years catching up with itself. And when I considered too the divorce your parents had been through, and the fairly turbulent life you experienced in your early years, I thought that perhaps it wasn't so surprising that you had a certain distrust of life.

But the restraint, the half-heartedness, never went away. Instead, it increased – right up through elementary school and high school and further through college and beyond. For many years now you have led your adult life, which you have continuously perfected and developed to astonishing heights. The life you lead is the envy of all. But no one would envy it if they knew better, for it is a half-hearted life, devoid of happiness. You never seem to be fully and completely present in life. Your secret, backwards-looking eye has grown and grown, and today it seems that you almost see through this eye exclusively. You live in restraint's double-vision of nervousness, ulterior motives and escape plans. The stability and the presence which characterises the fully grown-up person never seem to have taken hold in you. Your nervous childhood has instead continued into your adult life.

✳✳✳

I would like to try to write about your condition. And as I said, I will attempt to describe how your condition seems, to me, to be linked to the self-understanding you live by. I will attempt to describe how, by virtue of your self-understanding, you have made yourself into the very opposite of what you truly ought to be. Of course, I will certainly need to talk about what you 'ought to be' from the perspective of my own field, that is to say, Christianity. But if you will try seriously to understand what I have to say, I promise in return that I will go no further than speaking about things that should be comprehensible to you on your own terms. I'm not out to sell you the glory of heaven or the grand systems of the theologians. I will speak about things that are of pressing importance in *your* particular world. Just how far I am in a position to help you with these things is another question. My future writings will perhaps come closer to answering this question, but in the end you are the one who is going to answer it.

I will write no more now, and I won't write any more on this matter before I have heard from you. If you are willing to listen to what I have to say, I will continue these letters, but I'll await an answer from you before I write my next letter. If you would rather be free of all this, if you can't be bothered listening to a retired priest who misses preaching to his congregation, then I won't trouble you further. If, moreover, you find my approaching you in this way inappropriate, then I ask you – sincerely – to excuse my intrusion.

Warmest regards,
Morten

PART 1

THE WAY YOU LIVE

Dear Rasmus,

Thanks for the call yesterday. I was more pleased to get it than I perhaps let on at the time. After I'd sent you the letter the day before yesterday I seriously began to doubt the whole enterprise. I couldn't see how my letters could look like anything other than an insult to your eyes, and I became more and more doubtful whether anything I'd written had made any sense at all. I slept badly, and would probably have had a small breakdown myself if you hadn't called and calmed me down. It was good to hear you hadn't taken the letter the wrong way. That it had, moreover, made good sense to you was more than I could have dared to hope. Thank you so much! I'll attempt to repay your goodwill as best as I can, by taking the next step in my writings.

After you called, Agneta and Alexander also paid an unexpected visit. They have been here a few times over the last few months, but it had been quite a while since I had seen them. They just came by for a cup of coffee and had to head off to an appointment in town. However, this meant I got to watch Alexander while Agneta went on her own to the meeting. He's grown a lot, and is becoming more and more entertaining to be with. We played with the little selection of toys that I still have lying around from Lene and Margrethe, and spent a fun hour together; then he suddenly fell asleep and stayed that way until Agneta came back. He seems to be doing well. The same goes for Agneta. She still seems weakened, more unsure and hesitant than I've previously known her to be. The last few months have obviously taken their toll on her – your collapse more than anything else, I think. But she seems to be getting by from day to day, and her spirits are unmistakably still there, somewhere behind her tired exterior. I asked her to say hello to you for me, so perhaps she will, one of these days.

But let me get down to business. In this letter and the one after it, I intend to say a few general things about how I understand your present situation. It will be helpful for the rest of the process if we have a reasonably clear starting point to work from. In my last letter, I wrote of the absence of happiness that seems to have impacted upon your life. The absence of happiness is, as I see it, the real and most decisive problem here, but this problem is no simple matter. It's linked, as I've already mentioned, to a range of problems in your understanding of yourself. It's these problems that I'd like, in a somewhat general and tentative way, to try to point out – in order, hopefully, to be able to give them a more detailed presentation in later letters.

✳ ✳ ✳

To put it briefly: your fundamental problem, it seems to me, consists in your never really seeming to have caught sight of yourself. You seem to have been moving forward through life without really seeing that it's *you* who's moving. You see lots of things, you see all the things with which you surround yourself and create your outward success, but you only see and sense *yourself* dimly. And so it has never, in a deeper sense, dawned on you that *you* exist, and that this creates a certain task.

Your concept of yourself is too external. You don't seem to see that you are something different, something more, than what we might call your 'identity.' By identity, I mean everything that you in an external sense know about yourself or can tell someone about yourself. Your identity is your conception of the role you play in the world. It's the sort of thing you're thinking of when you weigh up whether your life is going well, whether you are doing well, whether you're good enough, and when you hold up the picture you have of yourself and compare it with the picture you have of other people. Your identity is everything that can be compared to others. And while in a fundamental sense you haven't really discovered yourself and so can't really be said to be self-absorbed either, you are instead infinitely absorbed with your identity or your self-conception. But that's quite clear, for if you have no concept of yourself other than your identity, how *could* you avoid being infinitely absorbed in that very identity?

There are no limits to how absorbed you can become in thinking about how well that image you make of yourself corresponds to your dreams and ideals – and even more importantly, absorbed in how well that image stands up compared to the images you make of other people.

When you have nothing other than your identity, then there are no criteria for success in life other than the ones you get from comparing yourself to others. Life then becomes an endless and vain struggle to outdo each other. And it's a struggle that has no winners. It drains life, like an endless downward spiral that cancels out all possibility of taking pleasure in what's to hand *now*.

You've always been a champion in this struggle with others. You've always succeeded in positioning yourself in life in such a way that you became the one everyone compared themselves to. Your life became the yardstick for success. You had the best education, landed the best job and the loveliest woman. And you're certainly not without style. Your victories were never simple or vulgar in character. You are far too sophisticated for that. You always prevail with such refinement that the desperation that actually drives your work never shines through. And so others have seen in you not just the most successful person they could imagine, but also the happiest. My claim that your life up to now has lacked happiness might therefore come as a surprise.

Along with a career that has developed at an unheard-of pace, you have, until now, lived a supposedly happy life with Agneta. You jet off to another big city whenever it suits you. You spend time in your summer house. You eat out whenever you feel like it. You play the part of art lovers. You head to the Alps whenever there's a fresh snowfall. You hold party after party in your large Frederiksberg apartment. And these are all fine things, things that would be a part of any happy life nowadays. Understandably, they give everyone the impression that your life is utterly enviable. But it all has something forced about it, pre-fabricated, planned out in advance. It's always seemed to be an expression of plans you've made, and while you were busy with one thing, that secret eye was always peering in the direction of something else entirely: new plans, new victories. Happiness, here and now, has always been missing.

* * *

Don't get me wrong: the judgment that falls upon you here is indeed a harsh one, because it's a serious matter we're dealing with – but you're not the only person in the world that this judgment applies to. In reality, it applies to all of us. Only seeing yourself as you are on the outside is a universal human weakness. Even I, who present myself as having understood so much, have rarely been able to practice what I preach. For long periods I have seen myself getting caught up in superficial and vain understandings of myself. In my latter years there has perhaps come a certain tranquillity that has made it easier for me to avoid falling into this. But earlier, I was quite impressionable, and it's not so many years since I periodically found myself trapped in the same type of superficial self-understandings that I'm now criticising you for living in. So I hope you don't see in my criticism any claim that I myself – or anyone else for that matter – are above such criticism, but that you will seriously try to consider how this critique applies to you in your life.

In my own case, my last serious bout of long-term vanity and superficiality was probably when I spent a long period nourished by the belief that I was going to become a bishop. This one thought controlled me for a long time. I worked so hard and vehemently at this project that in the end I couldn't believe I was anything else than this project. Losing the bishopric election only made things worse, and after the election I spent a long time ruminating bitterly on the thought that I was *not* a bishop. When I think back to that time, I don't think I actually got free of that thought until Lene died. Her death gave me permission to think about other things, completely different things, and all at once the whole bishop issue became utterly remote and indifferent to me.

Ironic, isn't it? How many losses and defeats do we need to suffer before we stop falling prey to the simplest superficialities and vanities? If I'd won the election, and if Lene was still here, would I then have continued down the path of vanity? Possibly. In any case, there have been long periods in my life where I've been running away from the 'higher self-understanding' that I'm preaching to you here – until existence called me to order again with sufficient force. So I'm not really one to preach. But perhaps something similar is about to happen to you for the first time, Rasmus. Perhaps, for once, you've been called to order by the bitter blessings of defeat. Up to now you've always simply won. Up to now you've never suffered a defeat you couldn't replace with an even greater victory. But this time, I think, *this* time perhaps you've been hit so forcefully that you won't be able to just shake it off.

I'll let that question stand for now. I have to run for a few hours, but I'll return to you later today.

Morten

To my nephew – an insecure overachiever

At the consulting firm where you worked before you left to go to the Finance Ministry, they had an expression for people like you which I've thought about often. It's stuck in my mind because its precision astonished me the first time I heard it, and because it gave me hope that people like you might, after all, be able to figure life out in the end. My reasoning was that if, even in your busy world of commerce, you still had the time and ability to come up with such a precise understanding of yourselves as seemed to be contained in that concept, then you would also be able to save yourselves along the way. But I've since become doubtful about that last point, and I've also come more and more to doubt whether you ever even understood the depth of that concept at all. Maybe I've actually just read too much into it. But even so, it's a remarkable concept: you called people like yourself *insecure overachievers*.

You brought this concept up one day when you were telling me about the different 'types' that worked in the firm. You said that one thing you all had in common was that in addition to being the best of the best in your age cohorts, you were also both over-ambitious in life and completely insecure, terrified that your ambitions would not be realised. You said that you – half-jokingly – used the concept of 'insecure overachievers' whenever you had to describe yourselves. Fine, I thought, great concept.

But have you really considered what that concept means? I mean, if it really applies to *you*? Have you considered the uncanniness that arises when you try to think that concept through?

The concept offers an excellent starting place for what I want to talk about, and since you yourself are familiar with the term, it seems worth sticking with it for a while. The insecure overachiever must be someone who is fundamentally quite inconsistent. Such a person must have no stable or solid foundation to build upon, and yet nonetheless tries to build his way out of the problem. It's an impossible situation. You can't compensate for having a foundation made of quicksand by building a new storey on top. But this person takes no notice and hopes that the problem down in the foundations won't be found out if only the construction work on the top keeps going. He thereby remains in an endless panic, in a state of expansive growth that must never stop – because the moment he stands still, it will become clear that the building is sinking, that it is constantly on the verge of disappearing down into the insecurity it has been built upon.

The insecure overachiever must be the very personification of the modern order or, more correctly, disorder of things described by Yeats when he speaks of a world "turning and turning in the widening gyre" in which "the centre cannot hold." It's a picture of endless growth on the outside which leaves more and more chaos within. But the tragic thing – or the happy thing, if you prefer – is that no matter how much a person tries to build themselves out of their insecurity, the inner human experience of being something other, something more than what he has made himself on the outside never vanishes. Insecurity will remain brooding indistinctly beneath everything the person does. And it will continue to stick its head up in situations where the person is suddenly faced with an unwelcome confrontation with his self.

For a person *will be* confronted with himself. Again and again. He can't predict how it *will* happen ahead of time – but it will happen. It's an inevitable part of being human. One common description would be that it happens 'in the dark night of the soul,' when all around has become dark and quiet, and where he stands alone with nothing but himself. It happens in the moments where the things he normally builds his life upon seem to have vanished and left him bereft, where their rapid, superficial assurance of a beautiful order of things is no longer ready to hand. It's here that he confronts his own shaky ground. But this 'dark night' naturally needn't happen during the actual night-time. It can happen anywhere, anytime. And for the insecure over-achiever it indeed must happen, whenever and wherever – over and over again.

I'm reminded of a photo I took of you once. Perhaps you yourself remember the one. You must have been around four years old when it was taken; your parents were still together at any rate. Katherine and I had come up to visit you in the summer house. I don't remember where Lene and Margrethe were, but they weren't with us. The weather had been dark and sultry all day, and the beach trip we'd been planning hadn't panned out. A warm rain began to fall from midday onwards, just a few drops at first, quite heavily later on. I remember we sat in the living room and watched it rain. Towards evening your father had a phone call. It turned into a long conversation, and your mother stood at the door of the small office and listened in. After the call they decided in some haste to cancel dinner in order to go into town. I can't quite remember what the occasion was, but in any case it was decided that Katherine and I would stay back with you in the summer house. This was before you and I really knew each other, and you became upset when you heard that plans had changed. After your parents had left, I fought an awkward and unsuccessful battle to cheer you up. At some stage I found the camera. We took it in turns to take photos of each other until the film ran out. It's one of those photos I'm thinking of. You didn't cry; you didn't say anything, but just stood in front of the camera in state of uneasy loneliness. For one reason or another I've often had this picture in mind whenever I've thought about your insecure flight from yourself. This picture must have caught you in an early, and yet already quite late, dark night.

In adulthood, the dark night will often follow a disappointment or a setback in relation to the dreams a person has for his life. But in fact it needs no external occasion. One sees a person suddenly gripped by an insecurity which is beyond his control or understanding. An insecure twitch of the body, a chin that moves nervously as though it had a life of its own, an uncomprehending gaze that at the same time looks harried and apologetic. It's not a pretty sight, but it's the most natural thing in the world – as long as we're human. It's the most human humanity that bursts forth in these moments of bewilderment. Basically, I can only see it as a good thing that we are doomed, again and again – and regardless how hard we try to escape it – to experience our own humanity like this. But for the insecure overachiever such moments are anything but happy, for they undermine the conception he has of himself. These moments expose his life as a house built on the wind, and there's something heart-breaking about seeing this disorientation taking hold of him.

✳ ✳ ✳

Rasmus,

I have to stop here for now. It's already late, and I have a meeting in the Ministry of Ecclesiastical Affairs tomorrow morning which I also have to prepare for before bed — my leisurely life of retirement hasn't quite worked out that way just yet. I had hoped I'd be able to finish this letter today, but the subject goes deeper than I'd first expected. I'm sorry for the sparseness of this letter. I feel that I'm still having trouble getting a sharp focus on the heart of the problem. But it will have to do for now. It was important for me to send something to you today, as I knew you were expecting it. So you're getting a letter whose second half will follow tomorrow. But there should be plenty to read in the present letter for a start. Goodnight, and talk again soon.

All best,
Morten

* * *

Rasmus,

So, I'm back. Sorry for the interruption.

I've just come home from yet another soulless morning in the Ministry. It was more exhausting than it used to be. I don't understand how one can spend so much time on so little. But enough of that. On the way home I ate lunch by the lakes. Have you seen there's ice on the water now? If the frost keeps up for another week, you could skate on it. The weather is glorious. I hope you get a chance to enjoy it over the course of the day. Over lunch I gathered my thoughts again, so if the afternoon passes undisturbed I should be able to get the second half of yesterday's letter written. So, let me get down to business.

I closed my letter yesterday by talking about the insecure overachiever's moment of bewilderment, and would like to continue on that path for a while. In fact it was probably a stroke of luck that I took a day's break in the middle of the letter, because after I'd sent the letter yesterday it occurred to me that perhaps you'll find my talk of 'moments of bewilderment' neither new nor enlightening. You seem to be struck by moments of bewilderment again and again, but you also seem to be more than aware of this. By now you have many years' experience of what it is to be you, and over time you seem to have noticed that there are times when your usual strategies don't work. You know as well as anyone else these moments of pain, discomfort and confusion.

We've often spoken of this in recent years – and in future letters I also intend to discuss some of the attempts you've made from time to time to 'solve the problem.' So apart from pointing out a particular type of experience in slightly different words than you yourself would normally use, what do I actually have to offer that's new?

What I perhaps didn't make sufficiently clear in yesterday's letter was that what I want to awaken is not just an understanding that unpleasant or confusing moments happen. What I'm aiming at is to get you to catch sight of yourself. When one considers how you deal with life's uncomfortable and confusing moments, this sight seems to be blurred. You've noticed that life feels uncomfortable sometimes, but you've done no more than that. In the same way that I say you fail to catch sight of yourself, you don't seem to realise in a deeper sense just how much that discomfort has got something to do with you. You only seem to experience your self as something that suffers discomfort passively, not as something that has a role to play in this discomfort. So for you, discomfort becomes something that must be run away from, nothing more. But trying to escape like that is like trying to drown out your own voice by shouting, or a dog chasing its own tail.

Instead of remaining in discomfort and seeing what it has to do with you, when life begins to hurt you throw yourself into a myriad of diversions so as to forget yourself as quickly as possible. You head off to the Alps, you play sports, you play the art lover, you go out with Agneta. Or you anaesthetise yourself with work. And that's all perfectly fine. It's good for your spirits to "switch your head off" as they say, and to disappear into distractions. In that way you can forget yourself for a while and come out on the other side with a little more energy, a little more courage and lust for life. But this strategy is really just sleepwalking. You have just enough self-awareness to understand that distractions make you happier, and so you use them. But that's it. You fail to develop any more fundamental sense that it is *you* who uses them.

If you began to see yourself more clearly, you would be able to enjoy those things that you currently prop your mood up within a deeper sense. The way you live now, you take no real pleasure in your diversions; you just relieve the pain and call that pleasure. You swing between 'high energy' and 'low energy' as you put it, and you don't really seem to believe that life can be anything other than such a pendulum. Every time you feel a twinge of pain, you change position until it begins to hurt somewhere else.

Then you change your position again. Then when the new position begins to hurt too, you change position yet again. But being you, and being happy being you, isn't a matter of moving around a little every time life starts to hurt. It's about always *being you*, even when life is painful, and this "you" doesn't seem to be clear to you right now.

* * *

Allow me, even if still in a preliminary way, to go a bit deeper into this 'you' – and so into the question of what it is 'to catch sight of yourself.' I can easily claim that you've never caught sight of yourself, but what does 'catch sight of yourself' really mean? Clearly, such a term means different things in different contexts, but in the present context I'm getting at something very specific. When I say that you don't seem to have caught sight of yourself, it's your *will* that you don't seem to have caught sight of. To really catch sight of yourself as something other than your outward identity and success is to catch sight of your will – that is, to catch sight of what you, all the time and right here and now, will or do not will. The insecurity that lies in your foundations, and which always threatens to pull the rug out from underneath you, is a symptom of an undiscovered and unstable will. The will is the kernel of the matter and the real problem here. What I've said so far and what I will say in the following letters is all said with regard to this kernel. Here I can only give some preliminary – and perhaps somewhat abstract – descriptions of what I mean by this. But hopefully the nature and extent of the problem will become clearer for you over course of the letters to come.

What I've been calling your half-heartedness, or your constantly running on ahead of yourself, is at its most basic level a problem with your will. You never *will* wholeheartedly to be where you are. Your will is one long, aimless wandering from east to west. Kierkegaard writes, quite rightly, that purity of heart is to will one thing; and just that, willing *one* thing, is something you never do, for you're always willing a thousand different things at the same time. With you, there is no purity of heart, and so there is no true happiness in life either. Your will is never gathered together where you happen to be. For when you're in one place, at the same time you're constantly measuring and weighing up your present situation, thinking ahead and planning for the future. You're a thousand ulterior motives and forethoughts that are never gathered up. And when your will is spread out in all directions, it's also trapped in a downward spiral - the harder it finds it to pull itself together in one place, the faster it runs ahead of itself in the hope of finding peace somewhere off in the future. But the problem is in the here and now, not in the future. There's nothing wrong with your future; it's as promising as it ever has been. It's your 'now' that has the problem. To catch sight of yourself in this 'now' would be for you to catch sight of your will. For in the most fundamental sense, you *are* your will. The way in which you either *will* or *will not*, determines who you really are.

I'm afraid I've been speaking rather cryptically just now. Maybe what I'm saying doesn't completely make sense for you. But all I can say in response is that you should either: stop and slowly re-read what you've just read, or arm yourself with patience and faith that all will become clearer in the course of reading further. I'll come back to this question of the will later. Whichever strategy you choose, let me just say at the outset that what can perhaps sound cryptic or complex when described can be quite simple in lived reality. I'm not about to try to teach you some difficult theory. I'm just trying to point out something that's right in front of our noses – and precisely because it's right in front of us it can perhaps be hard to catch sight of.

So if you want to understand what I'm talking about, the way forward is not to learn my words by heart, but to start noticing within yourself how your will is constantly at stake, which is to say that *you* are constantly at stake. You are constantly willing one thing or another. You are always up to something. You can never get away from your will. Pay attention to it. Watch its movements. See how you are constantly willing one thing and not another – or, in your case, both the one *and* the other. And see how willing one and willing the other amounts in practice to not really willing anything.

If you have any hope of getting to grips with how you actually live your life and taking pleasure in how you live, you will need to discover your will. That doesn't mean that you ever could or should take full control over your will; life is multifarious and unpredictable and is always ready to carry us away. But you can start to train yourself to pay attention to the person and the will that you really are. Cultivate this attention, and a certain gathering together of yourself will start to take place. And just as importantly: to the extent that such a gathering fails to happen, your attention itself will help you see yourself with greater clarity –

to, quite simply, *see yourself.* The insecurity and chaos that makes up your foundations will then become less threatening. Then you'll start to see your insecurity and your dark nights as part of yourself and not just something to deal with by running away from them.

I won't make this letter any longer. If what I've said up to now has made what I consider your most fundamental challenges to be a little clearer, then I'm happy. I can't really ask for more at this stage. In the letters to come, I plan to talk about your history. If the challenges I'm talking about are still not clear to you, then I hope that by talking about how these challenges have left their mark on your life up to now I will make things clearer. It may well be a couple of days before you hear from me again. It's not entirely clear to me yet how I should structure the next letters, and so I may need a few days to think about it.

In case you didn't manage to get out during the course of the day, then maybe go out for a walk in the cool of the evening. That's what I'll be doing right now, before dinnertime. Have a good evening, and we'll talk again soon.

Best as always,
Morten

YOUR STORY

A Narrative Period

Dear Rasmus,

I think I've worked out how to structure my thoughts in an adequate way, so I'm ready to write the next few letters to you. As I'd suspected, it took a couple of days before I was ready for you to hear from me again. I also had to spend all day yesterday on a stack of administrative tasks, which delayed things still further. But, at last, here I am. As I said, in this and my following letters I'd like to write about your history. I'll try to show how your problems – as I see them – have impacted upon your life up to this point. What I've been struggling with is how I should structure my treatment of your story. But I think I'm ready now.

When I look at your life up to now, it seems to be characterised by three periods which seem relevant for us to consider. I call these periods your narrative, psychological and spiritual periods, respectively, and the following letters will deal with these three periods. This letter and the next will therefore deal with the first of these, your narrative period.

I've spoken about how you lack a conception of yourself as something more than what is connected to your identity. You seem to be possessed by your ideas about who you are and what you can say about yourself while, as I've said, your will – in the here and now – seems to be a blind spot for you. In this letter I'll try to write the history of your self-understanding. There seems to be a distinctive personal history connected to the development of your self-understanding, a history which has both influenced and been influenced by your understanding of yourself. Your story is no doubt reminiscent of other people's stories in many ways, and so you share your suffering with many people in this world. But nonetheless, your history seems in its own way to have incited and entrapped you in your very particular self-understanding.

As I've said, since your earliest childhood you've been unusually conscious of yourself and of how you compare to others. It never seemed to come naturally to you – and I'm sure there are good explanations for this – to go into life in trust and confidence that life wishes you well. You held back, considered and evaluated, measured and weighed. This aspect of you has always worried me, but as I've also said, for many years I hoped that in time you yourself would begin to display a certain trust in life. But the opposite happened.

In time you became more and more reserved, more and more detached and evaluative. It wasn't just your own abilities and inclinations that drove this development, however. In fact, over time the world seems to have systematically rewarded and incited this side of you.

While in your childhood and youth perhaps you drove this development yourself, as you approached adulthood the world itself seems to have set up a system for you to lose yourself in, where your flaws were admired and rewarded as the highest virtues.

Until you finished high school there was enough childish innocence and enough human companionship around you in the world in which you lived that your power – and desire – to orchestrate the world only won limited applause. Granted, you were always considered to be uncommonly talented and promising. But in your relationships to both your peers and to adults there was always the background noise of ordinary human intimacy that made your talents less noticeable.

It's perhaps both the blessing and the curse of living in communion with other humans that the uncontrollable mixture of love, expectations, hope and emotion which we're exposed to reduces the salience and usefulness of our particular abilities. But all that rapidly began to change when you got to college. It was as if you had suddenly found the platform you'd been dreaming of, a platform from which you could start organising life according to what was in your head. Here, noone knew you, and there were no criteria for success other than those you had mastered so well. At the same time – and this was really what I wanted to talk about – you weren't just given permission to live according to your abilities and inclinations. You were positively *urged* to do so.

You were encouraged to see your studies as the first rung on a very tall ladder. Career Days and CV workshops were held for all you budding economists, and one-on-one you practised how to describe and justify how your current activities fit into your future plans. I remember when Kathrine and I visited you during your stay in London, and how you barely had time to see us because you were the chairman of the Careers Committee – I think that's what it was called – and had to run a major event the very week we were visiting. Not that we were disappointed or anything. Honestly, we were just glad to see how well you were doing over there. Besides, we were busy being tourists: castles, museums, department stores, musicals, men on horseback, ladies with hats and what have you.

As I understood it, the event primarily consisted of students meeting experienced business leaders and taking advice on their career plans. In itself that was all fine. But to train *you* in making career plans must have been like giving a fish swimming lessons. I couldn't help but comment on the irony of the situation. But ironic or not, in those years you were given the chance to fully engage in and pursue your idea of yourself, and your path through life ever since has been one long, successful replay of that self-idea.

In the jobs that followed, first in the private sector and then in public service, the rewards for your ability to see ahead and organise life have been many. You swam on and on in these waters as if it was what you were born to do.

I'll take a break here and pick up on the same track tomorrow. Have a good afternoon and evening.

Morten

* * *

Good morning Rasmus,

Let me jump straight in and pick up where I left off yesterday: even though you swam like a fish in water, you nonetheless must have encountered difficulties along the way. Not difficulties with your career, but difficulties of a more personal sort. Sometime around your late twenties a change seemed to take place in you. I've talked about how you have experienced that life can sometimes cause you pain in a way that can be hard to manage. Things happen occasionally that you can't control. It was around that time, near the end of your twenties, that you became aware of such experiences. You began to see that your life was in fact never as easy, nor as painless, as you'd thought it would be. In any case, around that time we started to talk with each other about how life doesn't always work out as easily as we'd hope. You brought this topic up several times, and in fact I recall that at one stage you said that it was probably harder for you than for most people to find happiness in life. I remember that I enjoyed our conversations and took them as a sign that a change was about to come over you – a change from youth to manhood, if you will. You were starting to become clearer to yourself.

I can't say precisely what it was that set this development in motion. Most likely it was a mix of circumstance, age and experience, but no doubt it was also that you'd recently met Agneta.

It was as if meeting her – naturally enough – made you start considering whether or not you were really living the way you should. Whatever the reason, you started to develop, you started on something that could have led to a deeper transformation in your self-understanding. It looked like the beginning of something that I'd long hoped to see happen to you. But alas, this 'development' amounted to nothing more than a small hopping on the spot. No sooner had it started than it withdrew back into itself again.

That this development never manifested in any huge transformation is, ultimately, your fault – and your responsibility. I won't explain the poor result away. But I also can't help blaming our age for dealing you such a bad hand when you were perhaps ready to make a change. No sooner had you reached out for help than your development ground to a halt. While our age offers help in abundance to those who run into difficulties in life, this help often seems to consist of intensifying the disease that needs to be treated rather than curing it. In any case that's how it went with you. I remember how one day you came home to me and told me that you'd decided to visit a personal coach. Through a colleague, you had been introduced to this coach, a woman who had previously helped your colleague and who offered a form of narrative therapy. You deemed that this was what you needed. At the time I think I just said something along the lines of how it all sounded very exciting, and that I hoped you got something out of it.

Seeing a personal coach could in fact have done good things for you. But the program you entered into quickly brought your budding development to an end. No doubt the coach subjected you to this narrative therapy with the best of intentions. Afterwards you told me how you and the coach had first spoken at length about your life as it appeared to you at the time. You talked about which stories you told about yourself, and what other stories you might be able to tell instead. Then you spoke about which stories you would like to tell about yourself in the future. And you spoke about how you could begin to make changes in your life so that your stories of the future might come true. You've described how your conversations were structured around questions like: Who am I? Who do I want to be? Which life do I want to live? As I understood it, all this was repeated several times with a number of variations, the stories steadily increasing in richness and precision as the process went on – a richness and precision to which I probably don't do justice here. But can't you see the irony? The medicine you were offered only made your illness worse. You walked into these sessions caught up in your own idea of yourself, and you walked out again more absorbed by that idea than you'd ever been before.

Maybe your identity had changed its clothes and was now clad in the finery of narrative therapy, but deep down, one self-conception – or self-narrative – had simply been replaced with another.

The troubles in life that had first led you to contact the coach had perhaps been reasonably clear to you, but you had misunderstood their cause. Your own tentative diagnosis had, like the coach's, been narrative in character. You seem to have thought that if life could become unpleasant, painful or confusing, that must be because your life didn't look exactly like the one you wished for yourself. You must have thought that the error lay in your identity or your self-conception.

It never occurred to you that perhaps the problem was that you didn't see yourself as something more than your identity or self-conception. And the coach only gave you what you asked for. *Your debutante just knows what you need, but I know what you want*, she might have sung, like one of Dylan's women. She knew exactly what you wanted, and she gave it to you in spades. But she didn't know what you needed, and neither did you.

∗ ∗ ∗

In any case, this process actually did have a concrete result. Not the sort of result you had dreamt of, but a result nonetheless. One day, during your therapy, you said that you'd realised that the pursuit of money and prestige, which had been the hallmark of your career up to now, wasn't enough for you. You said that your conversations with the coach had made you realise that your current existence repressed a desire to do something good for your fellow humans. You were no longer happy just working for your own sake, you said, but felt a need to work for a higher cause. I must admit that this sudden community-mindedness caught me off guard. It was so much the opposite of what had seemed to drive your career choices up until then. But then, what do we ever really know of each other's innermost hopes and dreams? If you could become happier by doing something different to what you'd been doing up to then, then all well and good. Moreover, you'd certainly be capable of doing something for the common good if you set your bright mind to it. At this stage you must have been at the consulting firm for a good three years, and it wasn't too many months later that you moved to the Finance Ministry.

Now, you could argue that moving to the Finance Ministry wasn't exactly the most dramatic act of self-sacrifice for the common good the world had ever seen. But given your education and background it was a natural choice if, in a larger sense, you wanted to do something for society. So all told, this was a good thing. But as I said, it didn't seem that a deeper self-understanding had come about with this change. One self-conception or self-narration had simply replaced the other. All of a sudden it had become important to you that the stories you told about yourself had something socially minded or altruistic about them. You were now not just a successful young man, you were also a successful young man who did good in the world. It certainly sounded good, but if you'd thought this change would give you peace of mind, you were wrong. In fact you'd only increased the number of parameters you had to deliver on just to be satisfied with your identity or notion of yourself.

The endless comparison and competition with the world that had always imprisoned you continued. Of course, you yourself noticed that life doesn't simply stop containing moments of discomfort and confusion. But up to now you've kept yourself going with the thought that it's all just a matter of time; you seem to have maintained the narrative idea that when your identity or your self-narrative finally becomes good enough, then life too will be good. It would be interesting to see which dimension you'd add to your self-narrative next:

art, culture, politics, literature, wisdom? But you never find the one thing you really lack. You spiral downwards without end, and you'll keep doing so until you begin to understand that your real problem is your *will* and not your identity or self-narrative.

As your fundamental problem is that you never seriously, wholeheartedly *will* anything, because you are swallowed up in your conception of yourself, how could putting yet another brick into the grand edifice of your self be of any help? It isn't. But it seems to have been a fundamental condition of yours that up to now you've tried to solve all your problems in life like that. Your narrative or self-narrating period has, to a large degree, continued well beyond your meetings with the personal coach. And while you've managed up to now to live your self-narratives in a more and more refined way, you've also managed to get yourself caught up in greater and greater frustrations – frustrations which won't ease up until you really begin to see *yourself* in all this.

Talk to you tomorrow,
Morten

A Psychological Period

Dear Rasmus,

Your experience with the personal coach was the start of a long journey of self-examination, rather than the conclusion you'd initially hoped it would be. Despite all the work you'd done on your identity and your self-narrative, those moments of confusion, pain and insecurity kept repeating themselves. And once you'd bitten the bullet and started to seek help, it wasn't long until you also started to consider what might be offered from other forms of help.

Just over a year after you stopped seeing the coach, you decided that you needed to see a psychologist too. I remember you told me of your decision one day when we were sitting around at your place. That was when you still lived in Bådsmandsstræde. You said something along the lines of – and, in a certain sense, this is quite true – that the coach had helped you with some external things, but as life kept hurting, there must be something wrong on the inside as well.

You thought that you needed to work on yourself on several levels. I had to agree with you on that, because I did indeed think you needed to discover a different level of yourself than the one the coach had indicated. But nonetheless I didn't tell you that what you needed certainly wasn't psychological analysis. I was afraid that in your hands, analysis and psychological explanation would delay rather than hasten your really catching sight of yourself and getting on with life. Maybe I should have said something. Maybe. There are many things we perhaps should have said to each other. But it could well be that my fear was misplaced, and in these sorts of matters it's rare that we properly understand what we say to each other anyway.

There are things each of us must discover when we're ready, and I don't think it would have made any difference if I'd made my views known at that time. And of course I'm not sure that it will make any difference now either.

***

But let us see what happened during your time in the care of the psychologist. Or rather, let me attempt to describe what happened based on what you told me. If I go too far astray please let me know. From what I understood, it was one of your friends who had put you onto the psychologist – a middle-aged woman who had her practice not that far from where you lived. It had been a couple of years since you'd first contacted the coach, and so you already had a degree of experience with self-analysis so you didn't come to the psychologist wholly unprepared. It was clear to you that what you needed the psychologist to help you with wasn't more external story-telling – that aspect of you was as polished as it could be. Instead, the psychologist could help you to understand why you still struggled with a more fundamental insecurity that couldn't be narrated away. From what you said, I understood that you both tried to address this insecurity as directly as possible, and that you, in a fairly classic psychological way, sought to understand whatever it was that lay hidden in your developmental history that made you insecure. I believe you spoke about many things, and that the psychologist was in no way lacking in nuance or locked into a particular view of how things were. This was no simple developmental history you laid out; as a piece of psychological work it was surely as rich and nuanced as it could be.

Naturally, the themes that seems to have played a large role in your conversations was your mother. I don't know exactly what the outcome of that was, but it was a recurring theme of yours back then that your mother's political projects and ambitions during your childhood had cast a shadow over your relationship. It's possible you'd said something similar about your father too, but it's your mother I especially remember you talking about. The somewhat overlooked part you had to play in her political theatre would therefore have been what laid the foundations for your insecurity – or lowered your self-esteem, as psychologists say.

It's possible there's something to all this. Perhaps you have paid a price for your parents' ambitions. Sometimes I got the impression that the enormous political energy and seriousness that prevailed in your home wasn't always accompanied by the same amount of love and ordinary happiness in life. But I'd advise you to be careful about judging your mother. It's too simple to see your insecurity as something she gave you. Or rather, she *has* given you your insecurity, but that's not something she could have simply chosen not to do. For she was insecure herself, exactly as insecure as you are. If you're frustrated in your attempts to get your self-conception to hang together today, it's nothing compared to the frustration your mother must have felt in her revolutionary youth.

In saying this, I don't mean to deny that she could have done some things better during your childhood. I say it because you have to see the patterns which you're taking part in when you blame her for your difficulties in life. Do you think she didn't blame *her* parents? She blamed them for everything. Perhaps not so much that they had lacked love, but more that they lacked sophistication. That they were just plain, uneducated people. She was ashamed of them and criticised them in every way imaginable for not being better than they were. On the deepest level, she was really ashamed of herself, but it only occurred to her late in the day that her shame and insecurity were really over herself.

This blend of blindness and insecurity which was going on here – that's actually what *you're* up against when you criticise your mother. And you need to understand that just as she never overcame it, but simply reinforced and deepened it by hammering away at the world, you too risk making the same mistake. When I say you should be careful about judging your mother, that's less about whether your judgment is fair and more about the net you trap yourself in when you judge. If you want to defeat your insecurity in a deeper sense, the way forward is to begin to catch sight of the insecurity itself, not to explain other people's part in it.

∗∗∗

But just listen to me, eh? Now it seems I'm the one who's getting ahead of himself. I'm babbling on and losing the thread. My intention wasn't to discuss your mother. The plan wasn't to discuss the specific analyses and conclusions you and the psychologist came to at all. What I wanted to talk about was the way in which you made use of psychology. When I saw how you used psychology, my fears regarding your psychological project were, alas, not dispelled. You threw yourself into the project with great energy, and encouraged by helpful and instructive questions from the psychologist, a world of new understandings quickly began to open up for you. Before long, the secrets of your psychological life and history were almost queuing up to burst into the light of consciousness. That bright head of yours and your analytic skills only needed a little nudge from the psychologist – after which they could take control and dig into your own underground like zealous moles.

Once you were underway with understanding the underlying dynamics of how you had become exactly how you are, there were no limits to what you could find out. Literally – there were no limits. One insight led to another, that other to a third, and so on. You'd struck self-knowledge gold. And the psychologist steered you with ease through countless analytic perspectives. Your descriptions of and variations on how the world had created your insecurity and suffering were innumerable. Apart from your mother, your father no doubt also played an important role in your analysis, but you and the psychologist roamed widely in time and space. Your current life also went under the analytic scalpel. And of course, I suppose I too was put on the operating table at some point. I'd be disappointed if I wasn't.

During that period, you told me many times how your sessions with the psychologist had opened up a wealth of new self-understanding, and it was clear – and to this extent also pleasing – to see that the exercises gave you a degree of renewed energy and courage in life. Things began to happen that gave cause for optimism, not least in your relationship with Agneta. The changes in your relationship that took place were no doubt essentially the results of your work with the psychologist. At the same time, they also best exemplify how you both used and abused your new knowledge about yourself.

Naturally, my impression of the changes in your and Agneta's relationship could be wrong. But your psychological period coincided with the period when I got to know Agneta better. She'd already started coming here regularly when Kathrine got sick. At first, of course, she mostly came to visit Kathrine and so mostly talked with her. But after Kathrine's illness progressed and she could no longer receive guests or even converse for very long, she talked to me instead when she visited. I know that Kathrine was grateful for the visits while she was still conscious. I was grateful too, but on top of that I was also pleased to get to know Agneta. It was only then that it seriously dawned on me how good – or lucky – a choice you'd made.

Getting to know Agneta was a bright spot in an otherwise dark time, and while the future seemed to be sinking below the horizon for my generation, I could take pleasure in the discovery that the future nonetheless looked bright for the next. I valued our conversations very much, and no doubt on account of the special circumstances, they often became quite personal in nature. So the impression I have of the changes in your relationship during this period come largely from those conversations. We rarely talked explicitly about you and her though – I don't think either of us would have found that appropriate. So the things I'm talking about were things that were said between the lines. Hence it's possible that I've misunderstood the allusions and suggestions that lay within what Agneta said.

You must have known each other around three years at this stage. While you'd gone on to become quite an established couple in those three years, and of course in a certain sense had gotten to know each other, it seems to have been a recurring and growing problem for Agneta that 'there was something closed up' about you. She couldn't have helped but notice your reticence and half-heartedness, and to her it looked as if there was something you kept hidden, some 'innermost depths' which you didn't want to share with her. She had certainly complained several times in the course of your relationship that while you perhaps talked about yourself a lot, you never wanted to talk seriously about *you*. You only talked about superficial things such as what had happened at work, or where you wanted to live someday or what you wanted to do at the weekend.

From what she told me, all that changed dramatically during your psychological period. A new intimacy arose between you.

Suddenly, you had time to talk about all the entanglements and developments that your life had now turned out to be the result of. Your relationship with your mother, your upbringing after the divorce, your lonely childhood, your school days as a precocious student – Agneta was now allowed to hear about all of it. When together you and she laid bare the innermost recesses of your psychology long into the night, it was as if the openness Agneta had always missed had suddenly come into being. You were completely open, you could talk right through yourself, as it were. You and she talked and talked. Or rather, *you* talked, and your talk was like drawing water from a bottomless well.

You'd started something that, once it had been set in motion, couldn't stop itself. Insight led to insight, and explanation led to explanation. And in your enthusiasm for not falling under the label "closed" anymore, you failed to notice that this endless talk was part of, rather than the solution to, your problems.

But by this stage Agneta seems to have noticed the problem. As the process wore on, her references to your project became less and less enthusiastic. At first she was probably just starting to get bored and was finding it hard not to lose the thread in your long conversations. But after having been bored for some time she must have begun to wonder whether this openness she'd sought for so long, and which she now had, wasn't what she'd wished for after all. But in fact it's quite simple: your talk and your analysis wasn't really openness. The analysis postponed *your* getting started on living your life. Your 'outward' storytelling had now merely been replaced for a while with an 'inward' storytelling.

In that sense, Agneta at first saw things just as wrongly as you did. She thought the openness that was lacking in your relationship was a kind of openness about personal secrets – the sort of thing the psychologist could help you to uncover. But authentic openness is something quite different. It's about willing, here and now – regardless of whether or not you've understood everything's deep psychological foundations.

Only when you earnestly *will*, with a whole and pure heart, have you started to live and thereby finished hiding yourself from yourself and from others. Only then have you really opened up or shown yourself. And neither psychology nor any other science can explain how you get there, because it's not a matter of *explaining* anything. You need to start *doing* something. But this 'you' is a blind spot for you. All you've done is expanded your narrative repertoire with a heap of good psychology.

Rasmus, I think I'm in a bit over my head with this letter now. I have some errands to do now and must set this writing aside for a while. But if all goes well I'll return to it later today and round off my description of your 'psychological period.'

Talk to you later,
Morten

* * *

Rasmus I'm Back,

By this point it had become clear to you that Agneta was no longer quite as enthusiastic about your psychological narratives as she
had been at the start of your psychological period. Tellingly, that
was pretty much the death knell for your work with the psychologist – after all, what use is psychology to you if there's no audience?
Who wants to tell stories if there's no-one to listen? I got the impression that your interest in psychology had quietly ebbed away,
without your coming to see why that interest was always bound
to fade – why psychological analysis couldn't solve your problems.
In any case I noticed that you gradually brought up psychology
less and less, until eventually your psychological period seemed to
have subsided altogether. In another letter, I'd like to come back
to the question of psychology. For while it was good that you set
it aside, given the way you'd used it, psychology also contains possibilities which, even if they were lost on you the first time around,
might be better made use of another time. But more on that later;
for now I'll bring this letter on your psychological period to a close.
In the next few days, I hope to get through a description of what I
call your spiritual period. We'll just have to wait until the day after
tomorrow to see whether or not I succeed. Hopefully I'll be able to
get it done before the weekend. But in any case – thanks very much
for your attention up to now, and to what's shortly to come.

Have a good night,
Morten

A Spiritual Period

Dear Rasmus,

When the enthusiasm of your psychological period had died down,
it wasn't very long before you noticed that you hadn't made any real
progress. The insecurity, unease, and confusion must have continued
to come crashing in over you, unannounced and unwelcome, the moment you weren't absorbed in your various projects. I don't know exactly
how long things went on like that, but I got the impression that for a
while you set the struggle aside and let life go along as best it could. In
any case, you didn't talk about any new attempts to work on yourself for
some time – until, one day you announced that you'd begun meditat-
ing. That must have been almost two years ago. If I remember rightly,
we were sitting in Nyhavn, drinking coffee in the early spring sunshine,
when you unveiled the newest instalment in your self-development
history. Needless to say, I hadn't seen that coming. You'd managed
to take me by surprise yet again. You'd never given any hint of being
interested in that sort of thing before. But your flirtation with the
spiritual also turned out to be short-lived.

61

Even though it was an unusual move for you to take up meditation, there was in fact a certain logic in your reaching this as the zenith of your development history to that point. I've said again and again that your problem is your will, which in a certain sense is to say your *being-there*, being present here-and-now, and that sense of being-there is precisely what meditation works on. In contrast to your narrative and psychological analyses, this was a matter of doing real work on *yourself*. That you had come to the realisation that this is where the battle had to be fought if you were to have any hope of fundamentally improving your life was, in itself, good news. I don't know who had put you onto meditation, but either way, you'd found your way to a centre in Østerbro where meditation, yoga and various form of asceticism were practiced, apparently to a high level.

From what I understood, the disciplines practiced in the centre were amalgams of various Eastern traditions. I can't say if mixing them up like that was a good thing, but then my impression is that the spirituality we import from the East always comes in a somewhat mixed form anyway – probably because it's always more economical to bundle together things you're shipping long-distance. But whatever the case, you'd started going to meditation classes, and shortly afterwards you started to take regular yoga classes at the centre too. It was interesting to hear you talk about your experiences with both meditation and yoga. But even more interesting – and surprising – was seeing the development that really did start to happen to you. Your earlier narrative and psychological projects had given you more to talk about, perhaps, but had no effect on how you lived your life; but the meditation and yoga did make a difference. You suddenly seemed to have, if not control over your will and thoughts, then at least a greatly heightened awareness and consciousness of how they ran away with you. That's what you said, anyway, and when I looked at you, it seemed that really was in fact the case.

You weren't like you were before, tangled up in all your plans and worries. Instead you seemed to have taken a step back from yourself, and had found rest – and even a certain pleasure – in letting go of everything that had been you up to then, so as to be present here and now 'in a purer form' instead. Of course I'm borrowing your own words and descriptions, but they suit the state you seemed to be moving towards. When, for instance, we spent time at the summer house at the start of that summer, the days came and went with a very different kind of peace than I was used to on our trips. Those days still seem to me to have had a particular nuance and clarity which seems at once both very fine and very strange.

However surprising it was to see you begin to undergo this type of development, it was just as surprising to see how, a few months later, you suddenly decided to drop the whole thing overnight. You said you'd come to the conclusion that the whole thing was all a bit spooky – your words – and that you would rather lead your regular, frustrated life than to lose everything in exchange for a spiritual dreamland. Once again, I hadn't seen your decision coming at all. Even though I hadn't really thought you were suited to higher forms of spirituality to begin with, I'd thought you would nonetheless hang in there, as it seemed to be having a positive effect on you.

As I said, I don't know which types of meditation or yoga were practiced in the centre that you'd found. My knowledge of meditation and yoga is pretty limited overall. But nonetheless, I believe that you did the right thing in stopping. Without knowing precisely what went on in the centre, in principle I have a few reservations – or maybe rather concerns – about the spirituality that seems to be on the market these days. Not so much because of the superstition that tends to accompany spirituality; that sort of thing will probably always exist and doesn't really do any serious harm. My worry concerns the consciousness-raising exercises such as meditation and yoga that are sold to highly talented, highly ambitious and frustrated people like you. It's their practice of the 'now' that worries me. The being-present-here-and-now that they idealise is, as a rule, distant and detached. To my mind it's not really human. But I should probably say a little more about all that. For given that I've been saying all along that you need to catch sight of your own will, and as meditation or yoga work on just that level, how can I see them as leading you astray? Maybe you can ponder what the answer to that question might be while I take a short break from writing.

I'll be back soon with my attempt at an answer.
Morten.

⁕

Good evening Rasmus,

(Continued from the last letter). The problem is that every spiritual movement that has discovered the will – and has thereby also discovered just how malleable and changeable the will is – tends to cultivate the will in inappropriate and overblown ways. Both within Christianity and outside it, different forms of spirituality, Stoicism and mysticism have sprung up from time to time over the last two thousand years. And where they haven't arisen in an organised and visible form, they've still always been there, as an undercurrent to the main tendencies in Christianity. What these undercurrents and movements have had in common has typically been the idea that through special processes of cleansing and perfecting the will, a person can come to share in higher forms of life – which in the Christian version means that the person can thereby become closer to God.

This sort of thing can of course sound enticing, but in my view, beliefs and practices like this are both unchristian and inhuman. Adherents of these movements become annoying at a high level. They have discovered that if they work on themselves doggedly enough they can put themselves beyond the reach of life's filth, struggle, and strife, and at the same time they have come to think that this very aloofness makes them specially favoured in God's eyes.

In Christianity, the latter is a grave sin, based upon the unwarranted assumption that one can work out what God wants here in life. And from this unwarranted assumption one draws the no less unwarranted conclusion that what God wants is for us to harden ourselves and make ourselves untouchable by the life we've been given. No doubt many psychological and historical explanations could be given for this type of belief, but nonetheless, it's dangerous. It reduces God to an idol which one can control through a kind of spiritual technical skill.

Maybe I'm getting into some theological considerations here that might not interest you, but the theology goes hand in hand with the human side of the problem. Looked at in human terms, the problem is that people in these sects and movements begin to perfect themselves and on the deepest level want to have themselves all to themselves. They no longer want life and all that it involves. They shut themselves in and become self-satisfied. While it's true that I called this a human problem, strictly speaking it's a human-Christian problem. For even though it's not directly a theological problem, it's Christianity that recognises such a practice as problematic. Christianity is the sworn enemy of this type of practice.

Paul Tillich describes with great accuracy how Stoicism was early Christianity's true enemy, while Christianity's direct political opponents – such as the emperors Nero and Julian – were not essentially Christianity's enemies. Christianity can survive just so long as there is struggle in life. But when a person uses his self to resign from life, then in a fundamental sense he does the very opposite of what Christianity asks.

For these reasons I'd rather see you – forgive me for saying this – confused and unhappy in your narrative-hungry, identity-hungry life, than happy in a detached, meditative one. As long as you're struggling madly like some latter-day Nero to see your life-projects through to the end, you are, in spite of everything, still *in* life, and there's still a chance that one day I'll be able to get through to you. But if you've already let yourself be driven away into a self-sufficient spirituality, Stoicism or mysticism, you'll quickly end up so far out to sea that you won't be able to hear me no matter how loudly I shout.

But when I say that *I* would rather see you unhappy in this life than happy in a distant and unreal life, I'm really just repeating what you yourself have said. You yourself gave up your spiritual projects for this reason. So don't take my Christianity-talk here as anything other than an attempt to point out an understanding of life that we – you and I – share with each other, despite our different standpoints, an understanding that seems to come through regardless of whether we happen to be avowed Christians or not. Later, I'd like to return to the question of which fundamental life-understandings we seem to share with each other. But it won't be in this letter – so bear with me. I'll stop here while this letter can still get to you in time to be your evening lecture. You'll hear from me again tomorrow.

All best,
Morten

On Will

It's finally become necessary for me to say something more about the will. I've said that you need to become whole-hearted here and now, and at the same time I've criticised various spiritual schools as abuses of the will. But what do I really mean by 'will'? It's time I tried to say something about this. Perhaps, while reading, you've also gradually become impatient over my unexplained use of this term. In any case you've now asked several times about the significance of 'will.' So let me here try to explain – at least in outline – what I understand by this term.

By will, I mean *a person's entire fundamental stance or orientation.* Perhaps that sounds abstract, but the fact is that "will" can never be described very precisely, because the will is the term I use for the *whole* person's way of relating to the world. So it's not simply one characteristic or ability alongside a person's other capacities. The very idea of such a collective term for a person's way of being first arises with Christianity – and possibly more or less simultaneously with it in various forms of Stoicism. I won't waste time on this history, as I'm no historian anyway, and there's a risk that I'll say the wrong thing. But what I want to point out with this historical commentary is that the idea of the will can, with some justification, be said to have developed in and with Christianity. And that makes sense, because precisely what Christianity wants is the *whole person.*

When Christianity comes into the world, it doesn't just want to get hold of rational beings or citizens, but of the whole person, boots and all. In other words, the will is *the thing one preaches to*, and will is something a person must show rather than some 'objective' or 'biological' property of the person. As such, the will is not something you have, but something you must do. When Christianity preaches, for example, 'love thy neighbour,' the right answer to this is a will-answer. It's not enough to say that you've understood the commandment or that you approve of it in some vague sense – no, the only appropriate answer to such a command is to actually love the neighbour, fully, totally and with your whole self.

The metaphor of the heart, which I myself make frequent use of, is also a Christian matter. In Christianity we do not say that you must will something whole-headedly, but whole-heartedly, because this expression best captures the form of action we want to see in a person when we talk about willing. When a person wills whole-heartedly, the whole person is determined by that will. That also means that there is nothing 'behind' the will – there is no person who 'uses his will,' but the whole person is determined by and absorbed in his will. If there was something hidden behind the will, then the will could indeed only be half-hearted and not the person's entire orientation. In this sense, the will *is* the person. I'm not sure how helpful these somewhat philosophical points are to you. But the thing I'd like you to take from all this is that the will is a collective term for a person's entire stance or orientation in life, and that the person is actively involved in determining this stance or orientation. The person can in a fundamental sense 'organise' themself for good or ill – if a person misuses his or her will, he or she can simply turn away from life. That's not to say that we have or could ever win total control over our will, but it's in the will that the most fundamental determination of the person takes place.

Perhaps this understanding of the person as determined by the will has fast become very complex in its philosophical presentation. It shouldn't be hard to understand in practice though, because we still today have the same basic conception of the person as was introduced by Christianity.

A person who, for example, doesn't really *will* to be there with us, a person who is uninterested and seems rather to be somewhere else altogether, we naturally take to be a bad person – at least in the given situation. We say that his 'heart's not in it.' And that's really just what I'm trying to say to you: Rasmus, your heart's not in it. I imagine that Agneta must also have tried many times to say that to you. We are still today, in our modern understanding, determined by our will, and we see and judge each other on the basis of the will that's being shown.

The will not only determines how we stand in relation to other people; it also determines how we stand in relation to ourselves. And insofar as the will is shaped by the work we do on ourselves, we can influence how we are in the world and how we experience it. This is what the spiritual person, the Stoic or the mystic, is absorbed by, and that's why their characters are so frightful. The will, which had been a matter of how a person situates himself in relation to God and life, has for them become its own project and begins to perfect itself to such a degree that it's driven out of life – and, according to the Christian, away from God. That's a mistake. The point wasn't to make yourself untouchable or perfect yourself. The point was that you should come to will *in* life exactly as it's given to you, in its particular mix of sorrow, joy, and pain.

Despite my scepticism towards spirituality in its various shapes and forms, I should in fairness mention that Christian mysticism, for example, represents some of our tradition's richest reflections on human psychology. The person for whom the will has truly revealed itself as both task and problem has often found great inspiration in mysticism. Both Luther and Kierkegaard were inspired and influenced by mysticism – and no-one has seen more clearly than they how the will is a problem. No-one has seen and analysed how the will always falls into willing wrongly, into being self-absorbed or 'self-seeking' as it's called, like they have.

In the mystics' radical attempt to purge the will of human wilfulness and self-centredness, they must have found a kind of answer to their problems. But they didn't stop with mysticism, because you *can't* stop with mysticism. For as mysticism at its best is a process of eliminating self-absorption, it lets a higher form of self-absorption in through the back door: the self-absorption that consists in being excessively caught up in getting rid of self-absorption.

In his spiritual project, the mystic thinks himself too important. And this problem seems to me to arise again in modern forms of spirituality. So while there perhaps really is something to learn here, we have to take care that we don't learn too much.

Warm regards,
Morten

Rasmus,

It's already late in the evening, but I wanted to have my discussion of 'your spiritual period' finished today. So let me round things off on this topic here.

When I say that you need to catch sight of your will and come to will wholeheartedly in your life, I do so with the caveat that while this is indeed what it's all about, you mustn't come to will in a fantastic or excessive sense. You mustn't throw yourself into gimmicky forms of spiritual hygiene, but, quite simply, will to be you, exactly where you are. You must will to the point where your person, in all its quirks and brittleness, rings clear and clean – as itself. Nothing more, nothing less. My warning against excessiveness doesn't mean that you should only will in a lukewarm way, but that you must will rightly. You mustn't begin to wipe yourself out in order to find a pure and untouchable self. It's a fine balance, and you'll never be entirely free of accidents, of leaning over too far one way or the other, but nonetheless, this is where the task lies.

I still need to come back to what was the starting point of the last few letters you've received – your use of meditation during your spiritual period. While meditation's more extreme tendencies clearly scared you off, and while I'm also sceptical about it, there was still a possibility that you could have gotten something more and better out of meditation than you actually did. I say that because if the meditation really could have a beneficial effect on your life, then it's not up to me to take such a tool away from you. Just as I wouldn't take your job, your skiing, your jet-setting or anything else from you, neither would

I take your meditation away from you. I'm not out to impose negative rules on your life. It's your life, and it can be good in many different ways and contain many different kinds of things.

I react against certain life-views or ways of living when I see a particular aspect of life raised up and worshipped – the adherents think they're 'onto something big here' – when in fact they lock themselves in and diminish life. It says something important about you, and about the insecurity that seems to brood in you, that your narrative, psychological and spiritual periods all ended up in one-sided and extreme forms of practice. But let me just say in closing that if you could find a more balanced way of practising the different dimensions of life, then even meditation could very well be a part of your life.

If practised in a balanced way, nothing is bad in itself – or good in itself for that matter. But such a balance won't be possible for *you* until you begin, in a more accurate and stable way, to be the person who lives your life. Until that happens, you'll continue falling into extremes.

Right, that's it. Period. It's way too late, and I'm about to slide off my chair from fatigue. I managed to finish this subject today – all well and good. But I'm afraid that this success comes at a price, that I travelled a little too fast over too great a distance. But that's how it has to be. I hope you've been able to make head or tail of these last few days' letters. You'll hear from me tomorrow.

Goodnight.
Morten

A Narrative Period, Once Again

Dear Rasmus,

I'll be taking a break from writing over the next few days. My previous letters have been quite comprehensive, and we could probably both use a little break from thinking. I certainly could, anyway. Besides, it's the weekend now, and I'm having company over today and tomorrow, so I'd better start getting ready soon. You and your mother are coming over tomorrow, and I'm looking forward to seeing you both. I don't think we've all been together since Christmas. It probably goes without saying, but I'd suggest we don't bring up the topic of this correspondence. Your mother is always displeased when she gets the sense that I'm preaching at you. Nothing good will come for any of us from spending the evening arguing over who should be preaching to whom. I'm also planning to invite a couple of friends around for a drink a bit later in the evening. I think your mother would enjoy meeting them – especially one of them in particular. But don't say anything to her, I don't know if they can come yet.

Incidentally, if you don't feel like having extra company and you'd rather it was just the three of us, just say the word and that's what we'll do. You're also most welcome to join me for a drink before dinner by the way. That way we can talk for a little while before your mother gets here. You're most welcome, anyway. Looking forward to seeing you.

* * *

This letter is just a round-off and commentary to my last letters. In the last few letters I tried to describe some basic features of the story of your adult life, and I've spoken of a narrative, a psychological and a spiritual period. But it hasn't turned into some huge coming-of-age novel telling the tale of your personal progression. No such novel could be written about your story. It's true that the way I've presented your history suggests a certain progression in your self-understanding. But that's a bit of a cheat, for the progression is only apparent. In fact, it seems to me that you've been stuck in the narrative mode the whole time. It's been a recurring theme for me that you're absorbed in your conception of who you are and the story you can tell about yourself – that is, what you cultivated in your narrative period with the help of the coach – and this self-understanding seems to have remained stable throughout all these different periods.

This narrative self-conception seems to be so firmly rooted in you that you can't seriously imagine any form of self-development other than working on your self-narrative or identity. That is, whenever you've tried forms of 'self-help' other than narrative coaching, you've only done so in the hope that they could contribute to either refining your self-narrative, or eliminating the personal obstacles that are getting in the way of a quick and painless actualisation of your self-narrative. When you've experienced discomfort or confusion in life, perhaps you've eventually come to understand that this was something you needed to pay attention to and work on. But in a deeper sense you don't seem to have grasped that you must pay attention to these types of experiences because they have something to do with *you*. You seem merely to have understood that the experiences could undermine the plans you'd made in life – plans for your career and for your life with Agneta. You've understood that at some stage they could pull the carpet out from underneath you and your plans. That's why you tried to do something about them – and why the results of your efforts were so poor.

You made psychology into yet another chapter in the many accounts you're able to give of yourself. It never occurred to you that you could have used psychology for something other than to present the story of yourself. So naturally enough, when there was no longer someone to listen to your psychological narratives, you lost interest in it. The same sort of misuse was evident when you flirted with the spiritual. This flirtation was brief, because basically you weren't willing to distance yourself from yourself and your self-narratives in the way meditation taught you to – it was just too foreign for you. Apparently you were just hoping to find there a kind of shortcut to living your narratives unproblematically.

Your case is probably quite common. When I see how meditation and other forms of spirituality are practiced by countless people today who, successfully and unhappily, are tangled up in their self-narratives and life-projects, I can't help but notice the irony of the situation: people want to be cured of their narrative suffering – but only when they're promised that this cure will lead to yet more success, yet more narration. But ironic or not, you have to admit, it's a health industry that knows how to hold onto its patients.

I say these things in order once more to make you aware just how dominant your narrative self-understanding is, but also in order to head off the problem that you'll probably try to misuse my writings in the service of your narrative self-projects. I don't mean that you'll consciously take my message and distort and abuse it for your own ends, but that in all likelihood you'll do so regardless of your intentions. Given the self-understanding you now live by, you're hardly in a position to do otherwise. Whether in time you will be able to do something different, whether my letters or the shocks you're currently going through in life, or something else altogether, will be able to help you towards a different self-understanding, I don't know.

Of course, there's hope for you. Plenty of hope, always, even for you. But be careful in reading further that you don't make it into yet another simple self-help project. Accept that I might not even be out to help you – because my idea of 'you' is different to yours. Read as if you don't understand, even if what I'm saying perhaps sounds simple or straightforward. I don't say that in order to make my letters sound like they contain some deep, cryptic wisdom – they *are* quite simple. I say it merely because you probably *will* misunderstand what I'm saying, and so you'll be best helped in your further reading by assuming from the outset that you *don't* understand.

It probably wouldn't help for me to say more; the wariness or caution I'm asking for is for you to show, not for me to write about.

⁕

As mentioned I'll be taking a couple of days off from writing. After having spent the last few letters discussing your history, in my next letters I'll try to return to describing your present condition – or your present *conditions*. Before long, I plan to turn from describing how you are or seem to be to describing how, in my view, you ought to be – that is, turn from describing your *condition* to what I see as your *task*. But before I get to that, I'll spend a little more time on your current state. I'll try to describe some crucial features of your condition which up to now I've only described sporadically or indirectly. But more on that later. See you tomorrow.

Till next time,
Morten

VARIOUS CONDITIONS

Self-Absorption

Dear Rasmus,

Thanks for coming over the other day. It was good to see you – and lovely to see once again how you seem to be back on top of things, or at least well on the way. I got the impression that everyone enjoyed themselves; they all hung around until very late at any rate. By the way, what do you think: do you think Klaus could turn out to be good company for your mother? I don't think you'd met him before, had you? That's really strange, as I've known him most of my life. However it's only in the last few years, now that we're both on our own, that we've started to see more of each other. Did you catch his comments about parliament? I think he'll end up running for office –

that is, if they don't decide that age is more of a negative with voters than a familiar face is a positive. So you'd both be colleagues of sorts in the government offices. We'll see.

I was pleased to hear that you can still stand listening to me. I hope that wasn't just politeness on your part. Or at least I hope that your politeness doesn't make you take my letters more seriously than you ought to. As I said, do take them seriously, but don't take them too heavily. You said you felt really struck by the letters. That's fine – just so long as you haven't felt wounded. I'm shooting neither to injure nor to kill. But as I also tried to say, the letters continue to cause me anguish. I'm used to speaking in church. There, God stands above me and those I'm talking to. It's not me who judges, and what I say presupposes God's love and forgiveness. Take all that away, and my speech becomes inappropriately blunt and intrusive. I hardly amount to anything more than what Paul calls a "sounding brass, or a tinkling cymbal." Take it away, and I've absolutely no right to talk to you the way I do. I don't have any solution to this problem. As I say, it simply keeps plaguing me. And I raise it here once again in the somewhat vague hope of forgiveness, and to implore you not to take my directness too heavily or badly.

It might be a mitigating factor, however, that I'll soon be finished dressing you down. As I mentioned, I'll shortly shift from describing your condition to describing what I consider your task to be. That is, I'll soon be finished with talking quite so directly about how I see you in your current situation. But as I also mentioned, before I get to that I would still like to try to deepen or clarify some key features of your present condition. In this letter I'll therefore speak of what I call your self-absorption.

I'd claim that self-absorption is a key feature *of* your condition, but in fact it's such a decisive feature that perhaps I should rather say that it *is* your condition. Self-absorption isn't one problem among others for you. It's inextricably linked with every problem relating to *being you*. Up to now I've described how you flee from yourself. I've described how you never *will*, wholly and completely, to be where you are, but always seek escape through your projects and self-conceptions. Now I'm saying that you're self-absorbed. That might sound self-contradictory, for instead of being self-absorbed, aren't you always caught up in trying to get *away* from yourself? But self-absorption is just such a self-contradictory phenomenon.

For someone like you, who experiences insecurity and discomfort just being you, it might sound unreasonable to call you self-absorbed. What you experience is precisely just the insecurity and discomfort, not 'self-absorption', and you might even in your flight from yourself see a kind of proof that you aren't self-absorbed in the least – that instead of being self-absorbed you're forward-looking, focussed and hard-working. But it's in your lack of pleasure in being yourself, in the continuous absence of joy just in being *you*, that the self-absorption lies. Your dissatisfaction with yourself is an expression of a self-absorption, a vanity, which always gets in the way of your truly coming to enjoy life.

By 'self-absorbed' I mean something quite specific, something which I hope to make clear in this letter. The problem, once again, is with your self-understanding – it's nothing to do with your being less 'nice' or 'sympathetic' than others in any simple sense. One could say, a little awkwardly, that you're self-absorbed because you're never occupied with being yourself, but only occupied by your ideas or conceptions of yourself. If, just once, you managed to be fully and completely occupied with being who you are, where you are, you would actually experience what it is to *not* be self-absorbed. But you're never occupied with being yourself just where you are, because you're always occupied with your conceptions of yourself. And your conceptions are a disease that's out of control. You're always thinking about whether you're good enough, whether what you do is good enough – and it's not just in life's troughs that these thoughts live in you. They live as a constant parallel track to the life you lead.

While you enjoy being with Agneta, you enjoy to a still higher degree the awareness that she is the loveliest woman, the best catch, in your social circle – and you shudder to think that one day that might no longer be the case. Last year when you were promoted after only a short time in your previous role, your happiness at the promotion was due more to the thought that no-one in the ministry had achieved anything like that before than to the promotion itself. You can't take pleasure in a moment of sunshine without also considering whether the sun has shone more on others than on you. In life's high points you suffer just as much from your self-absorption as in the troughs. But there's nothing remarkable about that, for when you live off your conception of yourself, there's nothing that can stop these conceptions. Success, failure, it all comes out the same. Success and failure provide an opportunity for various conceptions, but you can't conceptualise your way out of your conceptions of yourself.

***

Just as self-absorption has something self-contradictory about it, in that it's really about not being willing to be yourself, it's also self-contradictory in that it's always about other people. The self-absorbed person is dependent upon other people because he lives in a state of constantly comparing himself with other people. Or more precisely: he constantly compares his conception of himself with his conceptions of other people. So you stand in an eternal comparative relationship to life. You compare yourself to your ideal conception of yourself, and you get your ideal conception of yourself by comparing yourself to others. For you, the ideal is to be a little better than the others – comparatively. When the only concept you have of your success is comparative, then nothing can stop comparison from running amok. Comparison feeds on comparison, it nourishes itself by comparing and never settles down, but always throws itself into the next comparison.

How could you, with your self-conception, simply be happy when others are doing better than you? And when you do better than others, how could you do anything other than worry about whether the others will catch up or overtake you? You need to constantly assure yourself that you really are 'good enough,' and when thoughts like that are allowed to run on long enough, sure enough they'll find something that isn't good enough. Your self-absorption is a negative spiral. So long as you don't have a deeper concept of yourself, you'll keep drilling further and further into your self-conception. Like an over-eager spider, you spin an increasingly finely-meshed net in which you hope to catch the world, but end up snaring yourself. Your comparative self-understanding makes it infinitely strenuous for you to have anything to do with other people. You can't hear about other people's lives without thoughts about yourself getting in the way. When I see you confronted by other people's stories, I almost can't bear to think of the painful effort you must go through. One can see how you only need to have heard a few words before the thoughts begin to go to work on you. You compare yourself with what's being said, and work desperately to put it into a context that ensures you don't come out looking bad by comparison.

Situations like this must set in motion a large repertoire of contingency planning in you. In order to survive the comparison, you need to anticipate the possibility that the story the other person is telling you in fact ends well. You constantly need to be prepared so that the other's success doesn't take you by surprise. You must think ahead in order to avoid the risk of being left exposed, disappointed and ridiculous, when it turns out that the other does in fact have a story to tell that surpasses what you can achieve.

When your efforts to outdo the other through comparison fail, you nevertheless always find an escape route. Luckily, you've seldom been forced to use this escape hatch, but it does exist – it's modesty. On the rare occasions when it's conclusively and irrefutably shown that someone else has been more successful than you, there's no way out but modesty. When all else fails, one can always adorn oneself with modesty. In such situations, you show the most exuberant enthusiasm for wishing the other well. You not only congratulate the other person, but take care to speak enthusiastically about his success to your friends and acquaintances as well, so they can see your modest joy. In return for this 'praiseworthy joy' at the success of others, you'll reap a little praise yourself – at least, in your own mind. But fortunately you rarely land in situations like this. On most measures you always have the most success, and as a rule you've been able to find good reasons to feel immodestly better than others. As I say, Rasmus, I hope you'll bear with my directness, but also that you'll be able to recognise yourself in some of what I've said here. I'm not completely finished with the topic in fact, but I'll stop here for today. You'll hear from me again tomorrow.

Best,
Morten

＊＊＊

Here I am again,

If one were to talk about your condition in Christian terms, one might call it sin. Not in some superficial sense – by sin, I don't mean those misdemeanours and minor fibs you might be guilty of in the course of your day. These misdeeds and dishonesties are bad enough in themselves, but compared to your fundamental condition they're pure innocence. In your self-absorption you've turned away from life. Instead of being turned towards life, you're turned towards yourself. Herein lies the sin. You are turned away from life with other people and – speaking in Christian terms – from life with God.

This fundamental form of rebellion or resistance to existence is known in the old Christianity as a deadly sin. In fact, you offer a living catalogue of the deadly sins. Your self-absorption contains all conceivable forms of rebellion against existence: envy, self-pity, delusions of grandeur, pride, avarice, reluctance, joylessness, hopelessness. If you'd lived in the Middle Ages, you would have been put on a cart and dragged through the land as a warning to the people. But today you must be content with dragging yourself around by the nose, and with an audience that sees everything – except your true state.

In his youth, Luther struggled with his faith. He lacked trust in God and dared not believe in His mercy. He repeatedly complained of his distress to the monastery's older monks. He said that he was afraid that God was angry with him. One day, after having to listen to Luther's complaints yet again, an older monk impatiently answered him: *God is not angry with you, it's you who are angry with God.* If only someone would say the same to you, Rasmus! If only someone could tell you that God isn't angry with you, but that you are angry with God. You live under the notion that the world demands something of you other than what you are. In your own mind you perhaps merely try to live up to the demands – or criteria of success, if you will – which the world sets for you. You think that the world is dissatisfied with you, and you try to improve yourself so you can be good enough. But the world is not dissatisfied with you. You are dissatisfied with the world. You are dissatisfied with your life. You're dissatisfied with being you. Your dissatisfaction is invisible, and no-one ever hears you complain. But in your struggle to improve yourself and conquer the world lies the hidden complaint and self-absorption – and in self-absorption all forms of dissatisfaction and opposition to life thrive.

Morten

Worry

Dear Rasmus,

Consider this letter an appendix to my last two. After sending yesterday's letter I got to thinking that I still haven't yet pointed out a key dimension of self-absorption with sufficient clarity. I'll try to remedy this omission here. The dimension I'm talking about is worry. When I say that you are self-absorbed, I could just as well say that you're worried. Worry and self-absorption go together.

✳ ✳ ✳

Worry is fear of the future. Worry is the fear of everything that might happen to you tomorrow. It's natural for us human beings to be worried, precisely because we're created with an awareness of the future. We know that life is not just what happens to us right now, but that it will continue tomorrow. And at the same time we know that if we don't take heed and think ahead, we run the risk that tomorrow will bring misfortune with it. We are worriers by nature, you might say. But in your case, worry has been allowed to take over. With you, worry isn't merely one part of life, but has instead become your whole life. For in your self-absorption you're trapped in fear of the future.

As you're forever occupied with your identity or your self-conception, your life is all about developing or maintaining that identity or self-conception. And this development or maintenance is always directed towards the future. You're constantly turned towards the question of how your self-conception can be secured – that is to say, how you can stop it from coming apart under unexpected and unwelcome pressures. You anticipate the course of events in a constant attempt to make the future's possibilities dance to your tune. But you're fighting a war with ghosts: The enemy never appears, and is always on the verge of fading into the distance ahead of you.

I wrote yesterday how you can't even hear someone else's story all the way through before you've run off ahead, in an attempt to make sure the story doesn't end up showing you and your self-conception in a bad light. In fact, this dynamic applies to everything you do – which is the same as saying that you're always trapped in worry. You're always being taken over by fear about what the future might do to your self-conception. And the tragic thing about the situation is that the more you worry – the more you worry. Yesterday I referred to your self-absorption as a disease that's out of control, and the same can be said about your worry. For whenever you sense that your conception of yourself is in danger, that is, whenever you're worried, you rush ahead of yourself. You rush ahead in an attempt to control the future. But in the future, where everything is still possible and nothing is yet certain, for every danger you vanquish, ten new dangers are ready to arise.

In order to escape from this vicious circle you will need to realise that it's actually *you* who worries. Once again the problem lies in your view of yourself. You've never really discovered that even though your worries are clearly about the future, it's *you*, right here, right now, who has been overcome with worry. That's why it never becomes clear to you that worry can't be overcome by worrying, and you let yourself be trapped in your attempt to worry your way out of worrying. Just like self-absorption, worry has the self-contradictory element that because you haven't clearly caught sight *of* yourself, you're trapped in yourself.

In your struggle with the ghosts of the future, your own existence becomes at once both intolerably airy and intolerably burdensome. You let yourself get caught up in worry's nothingness, a neither-nor that is neither heavy enough to give you a secure footing nor light enough to set you free. You can never become free because you are constantly inside your own thoughts. And you never achieve real gravity for yourself because you are never present with yourself in the moment, but always spread out in your thoughts about the future. You'll end up going through life a wretched figure that can reach neither heaven nor earth, but which, in its anxious thoughts, is folded in upon itself.

Much more could be written about this aspect of worry, the way it locks you up inside yourself, but I won't try to do that here. Let me just say that it would please me to see you cast off your worries one day. In fact what I'd really like to do most of all in my writings would be to skip over all the descriptions, and just deliver a simple message to you that you mustn't worry: You must not worry —

simple as that. But when it comes to messages of this sort, things are rarely quite as straightforward as one might wish, and as a rule one must be satisfied with having come a little closer via a back route. There is one person though, who down the ages has managed to say what I want to say with unmistakable clarity. So take this quote with you to bed, and we'll hear from each other tomorrow. If you want to read further, you'll need to look in chapter six of Matthew's gospel. Until next time, goodnight.

"Therefore I tell you, do not worry about your life, what you will eat or drink; or about your body, what you will wear … But seek first his kingdom and his righteousness, and all these things will be given to you as well. Therefore do not worry about tomorrow, for tomorrow will worry about itself. Each day has enough trouble of its own."

Greetings from a worried uncle,
Morten

Exceptionality

To the exceptional Rasmus,

I'd like to write yet another couple of letters about your condition. What I'm thinking of saying something about – or at least considering – is how your self-understanding seems to be reflected in your specific self-conceptions. Up to now I've spoken about how you don't really see yourself as anything other than your identity or external self-conception. What I want to talk about here is therefore what, specifically, that identity or self-conception you chase after is. Nonetheless I'll just talk about a few basic tendencies in your identity or self-conception – tendencies which I haven't yet fully figured out, and my descriptions may therefore become a bit vague. But I think perhaps once I have pointed out to you these tendencies in your identity or self-conception, you will be able to see more clearly how you're stuck in them. I'll try to describe how your identity or self-conception always seems to be linked to the exception, the *extra*ordinary, and how, alas, you thereby end up tying your own hands behind your back.

It seems to me that there's an underlying tendency in your self-conception to resist the ordinary – a resistance against the everyday, the banal, the unpretentious. An enduring dream seems to dwell within your conception of yourself, a dream that you'll raise yourself out of the ordinary and become something special. The very fact that you are dependent upon and enmeshed within your conceptions of yourself is, as I've said many times, a result of your self-understanding. Because you don't see yourself truly, but only see all the exterior things you can tell about yourself, you're dependent upon your conceptions and stories about yourself. The very chasing of a distinct identity or self-conception is therefore your primary problem. Secondly, this problem seems more specifically to be in your striking out in opposition to the ordinary and chasing after the special and extraordinary.

Perhaps it says something about your era and your generation that identity-chasing takes the form of chasing the special and extraordinary. But just how far this is really the case is less important here. What is essential is for you to see how dependent you are upon the special. Everything you do is borne up by a hope that it will contribute to your specialness. It's borne on the hope that in success you'll find proof that you really *are* something special. I suspect that it's a natural urge in us humans to want to be something special. We all want to be chosen, to discern some higher purpose to our specific lives. You aren't alone in desiring that. But for you, who lives by comparing yourself with others, that desire turns into a desire to be something special compared to others. Your career, your life with Agneta, your various interests and projects are all examples of this desire. They make you stand out as someone whose life raises itself above the ordinary.

In general, your exceptionality-project has succeeded quite spectacularly. But I wish you'd begin to notice how life – your life – is diminished when you live in rebellion against the ordinary. It's diminished because you make yourself dependent upon a few very limited conceptions of what life must be. The everyday and the banal disgust you, and you opt instead for their opposites. But the opposites only make sense against the wider background of the ordinary. In fact, you merely choose small deviations from the ordinary, and blind yourself to how in a more comprehensive sense you yourself live quite an ordinary life.

You think you can get away from the large portion of your life which doesn't exactly lend itself to being recounted in exceptional and enticing terms. But you haven't gotten away from it; you stand right in the middle of it and just pretend it doesn't exist. In this sense, your blindness to the ordinary corresponds to your blindness to yourself. What lies closest to you in life is lost to you. But you're not just Rasmus-the-successful or Rasmus-this-and-that. You're also Rasmus that shops at Whole Foods. You're even Rasmus that shops at the convenience store. You're Rasmus who takes the garbage out. Rasmus who can't sleep at night. Rasmus the public servant who would like to be paid more. Ramus that draws breath and has a heart somewhere between his neck and his navel.

In this limiting of life that takes place in your worship of the special, you flee from the tasks and duties that life in a more comprehensive sense sets for you – and you in fact make your own existence dreary and banal. If you stopped defining yourself in opposition to the ordinary, but instead caught sight of the ordinary life in its full breadth, you would – I think – start to see how limited your own conceptions actually are. And what's more, you would begin to take pleasure in and wonder at what life contains in its ordinariness, rather than chasing your ideas in their specialness. I don't mean by this that you should start to look ordinary instead of looking special. You must not worship the ordinary in any outward sense. I mean that you must discover yourself as a part of an ordinary life whose features are far more extensive, uncontrollable and wondrous than any project you yourself can grasp or define.

What I'm saying is still far too abstract right now. I ought perhaps to specify more precisely what this 'ordinary life' involves. I doubt however that I'm even capable of doing so, and neither am I sure that any final specification will help you. It is your own attention to life in its "ordinariness" - not my descriptions of it - that you need. Nonetheless I'd like to try to describe more closely some of the fundamental understandings I take to be linked to the ordinary life. But this must wait until a later letter. Right now, such philosophical-sociological deliberations would only lead us astray from my real issue – which is you. So you'll have to settle for my slightly abstract talk of 'the ordinary life' for now. I promise I'll get back to the topic later on.

Best wishes,
Morten

Individualism Without Personality

Rasmus,

In this letter, I'll continue with yesterday's discussion of the tendencies that lie within your particular self-conception. More precisely, I'd like to speak about the form of individualism you seem to worship. The more I've thought recently about the self-conception you seem to live on, the more some things in this context have struck me as quite astonishing. But as I also wrote yesterday, these are things I haven't fully figured out yet, and which I can only try to point out vaguely. But then, I could say that about all my letters, so let's just cut to the chase.

In your struggle to escape ordinariness, which I spoke about yesterday, you live *against* rather than *with* the world. You define success as conquering the world, as being something special compared to others. The self-absorption you suffer from here translates into an apparently simple and straightforward form of individualism: your existence is all about you, and about what you can get out of life. You devour successes like a greedy child. No sooner have you sated yourself with one success, than there's a new one waiting to be devoured.

On closer examination, however, the individualism that's at work

95

here is somewhat ambiguous. For you are indeed fighting for yourself – but the 'self' you're fighting for is defined in terms that, in a deeper sense, have very little to do with you.

You struggle the way you do in order to actualise *your* self-conceptions. But if we consider these conceptions or ideas about yourself that you chase after more closely, it quickly becomes apparent that they're not your handiwork. You certainly seem to live in the belief that your self-conceptions are your own work, something you yourself have created. You believe that your individualism is your own. But the conceptions contained in your individualism are not something you yourself have put together. The world you live in has defined your individualistic ideals for you. Your 'individualism' is a collective phenomenon. The applause you get for your individualism is a collective phenomenon. When you carve out a career for yourself in the Ministry, when you create a happy existence for yourself in Frederiksberg, when you haul yourself above the common run of mediocrity, then you feel that you've conquered the world. But it's the world's ideas that conquer, not yours.

The fact that you haven't created your own self-conception is not, in itself, a problem. No human being has *ever* created themself. But there's a deep and strange irony in the thought that we live in an age and in a society which dictates that an individual must, with a degree of force, form his self *against* the world. Today's ideal seems to be the person who shows his or her strength by being more successful, happier, and more independent from the world than everyone else. I read the other day in *Berlingske Tidene* that newly-qualified economists nowadays identify more with pop stars and sports stars than with white-collar workers. (It was probably this bit of information more than anything else that gave me the idea for this letter.) It strikes me as ironic that we can cultivate such individualistic ideals *collectively*. And it's no less ironic to me that someone who follows the ideas of individualism – that's you – sees the realisation of these ideals as a victory over the world. It's no victory, it's just you doing what you've been told to do. In your attempt to lift yourself above the ordinary, you're actually chasing the most ordinary ordinariness of our time.

While it might seem natural at first to blame the world for becoming individualistic, one nonetheless ought rather to blame it for becoming collectivist. The age celebrates all the individualist ideals found in your self-conception: *you must become successful, happy and independent.* But these ideals are rolled out across the world in the conformist and collective delusion that this banal-successful *you* is your authentic person. The individualism that's in play here is impersonal. It represents a resistance to the personal; and while you believe, in your self-absorbed way, that you're creating yourself, you're actually destroying yourself – as a person.

The purity of heart, the collected will that would be necessary for *you* to, in a fundamental sense, step forward and show yourself, plays no part in all this. There's nothing in your struggle that really shakes you or makes you shine through clearly as a person. This is so because the struggle, at its heart, lacks conflict. There's no conflict between your self-conception and what the world asks of you. While the struggle might look intense on the surface, in fact it lets your true, personal self sleep undisturbed. You build a castle. No-one lives in it, but the people stand below the castle and rejoice in its beauty. And so long as there is rejoicing, you'll keep building, and so long as you build, there will be rejoicing. In itself, this zeal for building might be a fine thing. But it numbs you and keeps putting you off so long as you remain of the belief that in some deeper sense you'll come to show *yourself* in what you're building.

✳ ✳ ✳

Good, I'm done criticising you – for now. As I mentioned, after this letter I plan to shift focus from what I call your condition to what I call your task. At the same time I reckon the next letters I'll send you will become a bit more philosophical than the letters you've received up to now. As I need to think a few things through before I write any further, it may be a couple of days until you hear from me again, maybe not until after the weekend. Also, I hear that you and your mother plan to head up to the summer house for the weekend. That sounds like an excellent plan. Everything up there has its own stillness and freshness at this time of the year. I think there's even an inch or two of snow there right now. Enjoy – and remember to wrap up warmly. Talk to you again before long.

Warmest wishes,
Morten

PART 2

BEING YOU

Dear Rasmus,

So, here I am again after a few days of silence. How was your weekend? I tried calling today – did you get my message? My weekend turned out to be a quiet one: read the papers, a couple of books, met someone for coffee Sunday afternoon. I've had a bit of a late start today, so let me get straight down to business.

In my previous letters, I've tried to describe how you manage to get into trouble with your*self*. I've described how your concepts and conceptions of yourself get in the way of your enjoyment of life. And I've spoken about how you never come to will wholeheartedly to be yourself – because you live inside your ulterior motives, worries and plans for yourself. As I've said, in this and the following letters I'd like to turn from questions about how you *are*, to questions about how you *ought to be*.

I've only been able to write about how you get into trouble with yourself up to now because, in my opinion, I know of better ways of being than yours. It's these 'better ways' I'll try to describe in the following letters.

In moving from the critical to the constructive, or from the negative to the positive, there's nonetheless a danger that what I say will be biased and simplistic. So long as one is criticising and smashing conceptions, one opens things up, which is rarely harmful in itself. But when one begins to describe "how one ought to be" positively, things are almost bound to go wrong. This topic – how one positively ought to be or even *could* be – is bigger than, and essentially different from, any description that could be given of it. It's something that only exists in being lived, not in being described. So read what I have to say below with some caution. Remember that it points towards a reality that is different from, and greater than, what is written.

I say that I'd like to see you live your life in certain ways, but before I say more about these ways, it's necessary to say a bit about 'you.' As I mentioned, the manner in which you go wrong in life seems to have something to do with a deficiency in your self-understanding. If you don't develop a deeper understanding of what 'you' are, it will be useless to even begin talking about how you 'ought to be.' This letter is just such an attempt to describe what 'you' are. And let me say up front: the issues connected to this question of what you are, are some of the most complex and philosophical that I'll be presenting you with. That is to say, reading this letter will become a bit demanding. But I hope that it doesn't become *so* demanding that it becomes un-intelligible, and I also hope that my little promise that there will be easier reading ahead will help you keep your spirits up along the way. Furthermore, I'd also better mention that to be sure that I've said the right thing, I'll need to 'start over' at certain points and repeat things I've already said. I hope that I won't test your patience too severely.

∗∗∗

Looking at your life up to now, it could be called a protracted effort to *not* be yourself. You've been busy creating an identity which you could be proud of and tell everyone about, and you've succeeded in doing so. But we haven't seen much of *you* in all this. Your proper element, that which surrounds you all the time – namely yourself – seems to have made you uncomfortable. Like a fish with hydrophobia, you've fled into self-conceptions that have helped you forget about yourself. Of course, I don't think your various self-conceptions and life-projects are something you can or should give up. They're one side of life's coin. But the problem is that you have denied what's on the other side of the coin, which is the fact that it is precisely *you* who is the one living your life.

Even though you have denied it, the fact that you are you is something you're always confronted with. When I try in these letters to describe what 'you' are, I'm talking about this very confrontation – this 'something' which you never escape from. That you are you, and that you are confronted by what it is to be you, runs through all the various life-situations and projects you might find yourself in. To be yourself is, in this sense, more comprehensive than any project or any identity you can come up with – for regardless of what you come up with in your life, it's a given that in all this you must be precisely *you*. You can switch your projects and your self-conceptions with each other, but you cannot change the fact that you have to be *you* in all these projects and conceptions. And what it is to *be* you is something that is fundamentally different from the stories you can tell about yourself. It is something fundamentally different from the identity or identities you try to rely on in life. For being yourself is precisely about *how you are*, and not about your conceptions and stories.

In other words, truly being yourself isn't about developing or winning a particular type of identity or gaining knowledge about yourself that you can enjoy or adorn yourself with. In a deeper sense it's not about knowledge at all. It's not a matter of *knowing*, but of *being*. Everything that you can know and tell about yourself – about your past, your future, your plans for your career and your life with Agneta – is a crucial part of what it is to be you, but what really determines what you truly are is the way in which you relate to all these things. And how you relate to it all always shows itself in the here and now. It is only here and now, not yesterday or tomorrow, and not in your knowledge or your stories of yesterday and tomorrow.

That it's here and now that matters must come as unpleasant news for you, because the present has always been the source of your discomfort. Like a dog trying to run away from its own tail, you find the present unpleasant and wish you were out in the future, out in your plans and projects. Of course, this race into the future has the comical aspect that the future, when it arrives, always arrives as a *new present*, whereupon you must then throw yourself out into a new future, and new projects. But nonetheless this is how you live, and you can do it no other way.

You can't do anything differently because you don't see yours*elf,* but only your plans and projects. When your projects run smoothly, when they seem to be succeeding as if in a story you yourself could have told, the here and now is no doubt quite tolerable – because you can almost forget that it exists. In such periods you can live as if you are nothing more than your own future, while the present is happily forgotten. But as soon as a crack appears, or uncertainty creeps into your projects, and the future is not quite as secure as you'd believed – which means that you yourself are not as secure as you'd believed – your plans and projects come rushing back into your head, and the here-and-now begins to close in around you like a dense and gloomy woodland.

Like an ecstatic swimmer, you stay afloat just so long as there's a reward dangled in front of you. The moment the reward is taken away, you realise that it is, in fact, *you* who is swimming – and you panic. Suddenly, you become over-aware of your strokes. Suddenly, you can't coordinate your arms and legs, and you switch to a frantic dogpaddle. You could have just carried on as if nothing had happened, but the realisation that the whole thing is really about *you*, and not just the reward that had been held out to you, makes you lose your grip.

※ ※ ※

As I said, I got started on writing a little late today, and it's already starting to get late. Since I have a couple of difficult descriptions ahead of me, perhaps it's wisest if I stop here for now and come back to this tomorrow. By the way, I also spoke to your mother when you didn't answer earlier today. She said you had had a good time together up at the summer house. She said she'd had a stack of books with her, and that you read both Gabriel Garcia Márquez and Günter Grass. That sounds like a good, and rather cultured, weekend. Everyone probably needs *One Hundred Years of Solitude* sometimes up there in the snow. Though I hope that we don't end up making you sick of reading with all our gospels. In any case I'll leave you in peace for now. Have a good evening and night. You'll hear from me again tomorrow.

Morten

**

Good morning Rasmus,

Let me continue my description of what it is to be you. Strictly speaking, you don't want to be yourself. You want to be completely free from yourself. You only want to have your ideas and conceptions about yourself, and you have never really discovered that the 'self' you want to be free of is more than just a small, unfortunate mistake in life. That's why you're amazed and scurry away every time you come across it. In this way you actually lead a strangely ideological life. You have quite definite ideas about life, and when it turns out life doesn't match these ideas, you take that to be life's problem.

You're like the man Augustine describes, who first envisions the perfect circle and is then disgusted by the natural world because he can't find this circle anywhere in nature. But your job is not to judge life according to your own, arbitrary standards. The task is instead to start to see and will life just as it is.

If I'm to explain what I mean by 'life just as it is' more fully, I'll have to resort to philosophical language. In the present context, a philosophical account would say that the experiences you have of yourself, on certain occasions and to your great discomfort, are not in fact something you *only* have on those occasions. Perhaps different situations confront you with what it is to be yourself with lesser or greater force, but the truth is that you are experiencing and relating to what it is to be yourself all the time, without interruption. In philosophical terms, you are a *self-relation*.

The self-relation is constant; you can't do anything in life without also experiencing and relating to what it is to be yourself. While you relate to your various tasks and projects in life, you're also relating to the fact that *you* are the person that stands within these tasks and projects. So long as you're in the midst of life, you're also in your own hands. At all times you are played into your own hands, and at all times you do something with this 'you.' This is difficult and demanding – it's "angstful," as the existentialists say. But if we didn't relate to ourselves in this way we simply wouldn't be the creatures we are. For good or ill, self-relation goes along with being human.

When I say that you must start to see life just as it is, this is a matter of your beginning to see your self-relation – to see that you are in fact experiencing and relating to yourself all the time. I don't mean by this that in some superficial sense you should start taking yourself more seriously than you already do. I'm not trying to sell you on a new form of self-absorption. On the contrary, I mean that you must become *non-self-absorbed*, but you won't become like this until you really discover yourself and thereby stop being afraid of yourself. Right now you're constantly running away into your thoughts, ideas and plans, and even though this flight from yourself is a symptom of your discomfort with yourself, it's also, as I tried to say last week, a state of self-absorption. You're self-absorbed because you can't stand being yourself. To get out of yourself, you'll need to start really seeing and willing to be yourself, with everything that entails.

I'll take a break here for a couple of hours, but I'll be back later today.

Best,
Morten

⁕ ⁕ ⁕

Good afternoon Rasmus,

In my description of what 'you' are earlier today, I introduced the concept of self-relation. I'll continue here where I left off and try to speak about this concept in a little more depth. 'Self-relation' is a philosophical concept that, in itself, says little about the lived contents of your experience of being yourself. Self-relation is a universal concept that points to a particular cognitive structure connected to being human. However, by joining the concept of self-relation with that of *personality*, I hope to make the concept a little more real and recognisable

– to give it a bit more psychological flesh and blood – in relation to *your* life. While self-relation is a universal, and, as such, content-less concept, it is clothed in and coloured by the individual's lived reality, or what we call the personality. One could say that the personality is the *filled-in* self-relation.

The particular personality which each of us has is something that comes into being through a combination of certain individual psychological traits and how we, over time, stand toward and relate to these traits. As such, the personality is the result of a meeting between something specific that has been given to us, and the way in which we relate to this specific thing. It's both something we *receive*, and something we *do*; it is both passive and active. But neither of these two poles of the personality ever exists on its own. There is a constant exchange between what is given to us, and the way in which we relate to it, and the poles can therefore also change over time. Personality isn't constant or timeless. Just how much it can change, I don't know, but that doesn't really matter for what I'm trying to say here. What's important is to understand that your authentic personality lies in the meeting between something particular that appears in your experience of yourself in every situation, and which you must relate to, and the way in which you actively relate to it.

I've previously pointed out that your will is your real problem. In saying here that you are relating to yourself at all times, it's therefore important to understand that this relation to yourself isn't some neutral, intellectual exercise. There is will in your self-relation. While you're relating to yourself, you're *willing* to do something with yourself. You're up to something with yourself the whole time. And precisely what you're up to, Rasmus, is escaping from yourself, avoiding being yourself. The half-heartedness that is the hallmark of your life is a result of your wanting to get away from yourself. It is a result of your will, so to speak, pointing the wrong way.

As the personality involves self-relation and self-relation involves will, it's not unreasonable to say that you currently lack personality. Of course, you have various personal traits, just as everyone else does. But because you never really *will* to be yourself, no personality or character really shines through in you. Your race against yourself has blurred your features. Whenever anything that is *you* in a deeper sense begins to assert itself, you create a diversion. You run ahead and plant so many stories about yourself that eventually no-one – neither you nor anyone else – can work out whether they are really dealing with you or just with your self-constructed reputation that has preceded you. If you had more confidence in yourself, if you understood that you really are better than your reputation, you wouldn't need to race against yourself like this, but would instead just let your*self* shine through and become visible.

Greater confidence in yourself requires you to, in a certain sense, give yourself up. In order to come to really be yourself, to really be able to endure the experience of being yourself, you will need to renounce your own ideas about yourself. You don't need to give up your concrete life-projects; they're part of life and there's nothing wrong with them. But you must give up the notion that your projects and the ideas you have of yourself are what you *are*.

* * *

110

So in order to be able to start truly being yourself and shining through as a person, you must take your conception of yourself less seriously. In fact, for you it's a matter of making a confession, indeed, of undergoing a *humiliation*. It would be humiliating for you to give up your ideas and conceptions about yourself and thereby admit that you are something other than the plans you've made for yourself. That of course would mean there's something you're bound by, something you can't control, something that might not be beautiful or impressive or otherwise beneficial for you. You've been trying to avoid just this sort of humiliation your whole life.

Your life has been about getting rid of the bumps and obstacles that didn't fit the stories you wove about yourself. That there is something greater than your projects, something which can perhaps be concealed but can't be gotten rid of, must seem like a failure for your self-project. But the failure will only seem like a failure so long as you cling to your narrow self-conceptions. The moment you're ready to let these conceptions go, what now seems like a failure will turn out to be the greatest victory. For the life that is now half-hearted and in rebellion against existence will get the chance to transform itself into a wholehearted life in the world.

The psychological oddities and experiences that belong to you, and which you're constantly running into, are therefore not something you should wish to get rid of or forget, but something you should take courage, joy and pride in. But don't misunderstand me. You mustn't discover your psychology or personality in order to improve or perfect it. I've mentioned this before, and perhaps I lack confidence in you. But I can see for myself how, as soon as you're on the trail of some new aspect of life, you start to deliberate on how you can perfect it and make it into yet another project amongst all your other projects. What I'm talking about here cannot and should not be made into some project, because it's not something you can get control of – you can merely relate yourself more or less rightly to it. I don't want to contribute to any sort of 'cult of personality'. In what I'm saying there's no notion that your personality is anything especially fine or exalted that you should swoon over. I only try to demonstrate that there's a side of you – your living psychology or personality – which you need to consciously be aware of if you are to be yourself in any deeper sense.

I can't tell you in advance what your living psychology or personality would turn out to be like in practice. That's something that must show itself – for you. I dare say that you'll find variations on the full human register of anxiety, worry, deceit, enthusiasm, tenderness, intimidation, stillness, courage and discouragement. But the specific order, composition and strength with which the elements of that register will actually occur is something you'll have to experience for yourself, one experience at a time. But regardless of how they occur, regardless of which experiences you have of yourself, you must not explain them away as if they aren't you – precisely because they *are* you.

When you're suddenly shaken, and lose your grip on yourself because life hasn't gone the way you expected, it's *you* who loses his grip, and so that is how *you* are. When you're anxious that life with Agneta won't be everything you'd hoped, it's *you* who is anxious. And when you hope for success in life, it's *you* who hopes. When you worry about yourself, it's *you* who is worried. When you're overcome by enthusiasm, it's *you* who is enthusiastic. It happens to you, it's all you; and don't try to be anything other than the complex and unruly person that you are – but try instead to *really* be that. Be attentively and willingly present where you are.

I previously criticised your use of psychology in your 'psychological period' because psychology had merely furnished you with a range of new narratives and explanations, but hadn't sharpened your attention to what it really is to be you, in your living experience of yourself. Nietzsche is quite right when he says that in this day and age, when everyone has become scientific and is encouraged to seek explanations for anything and everything, the power of really *looking* has vanished. As soon as you encounter something unknown to you, you want it explained, and if you can't have it explained you want it taken away – you want it to simply not exist. But just try to *look at* what's there, look at what's going on, and take it in. Regardless of what you do with it, regardless of how you explain it – or explain it away – it will nonetheless be definitive of who you are.

***

I'll stop here. As I said, the last two days' letters contain a number of complex and extensive philosophical problems. These problems could be described both differently and at greater length than I have done here, and I won't pretend that I've understood all the details and nuances. But I hope that I've managed to indicate with reasonable clarity what, to my understanding, is contained in the 'you' which you 'ought to be.' If I've only pointed you in the direction of my understanding of this 'you,' then I'll be happy. I've certainly also said a little already about what you *ought* to do – for 'you' and 'ought' belong inextricably together. But in my next letters let me try to lay out this 'ought' further – and leave things here for now.

Warm regards,
Morten

DON'T DESPAIR

Dear Rasmus,

As mentioned, in this letter I'll be dealing with the question of 'how you ought to be.' Whereas in my last letter I tried to describe what, to me, 'you' seems to contain — what 'you' are — in this letter I'll continue addressing the question of what 'ought' means, and so how you ought to be. My previous letter was, so to speak, about *what*, while this letter will be about *how*. As mentioned, 'what' and 'how,' or 'you' and 'ought,' aren't two different elements, and so they cannot be treated separately from each other. But nonetheless in this letter I'll try to put the emphasis on 'how' or 'ought.'

You avoid really being yourself. You try to escape the fact that there's a 'you' that goes deeper than the stories you tell about yourself. Having tried to describe what this 'you' is that you try to escape, today I'll be looking at the evasion itself. In short, the 'ought' that I'll be speaking about today concerns that which you ought not to evade.

You must, so to speak, not *not* will to be yourself. Or more directly: you must will to be yourself. So when I talk about how you should *be*, this is about how you should *will*. And what I'm saying is that you should will to be yourself – at all times and without reservation.

As I've described to you previously, you are what you will. Your most fundamental 'how,' your most fundamental way of being, is determined by how you will. So when I say that you must will to be yourself, it's an 'ought' on this most fundamental level that I'm interested in. I can't tell you how you should arrange things on a more superficial level and what you must do or should do in life – I offer no such moral teaching. But your problem isn't on the surface. On a superficial or visible level, you lead a life that by all standards is both respectable and enviable, and I have no objection to the things you fill your life with. The 'ought' I'm talking about is concerns your fundamental stance towards life's content.

* * *

Let me take a detour concerning Kierkegaard and the concept *despair*. Kierkegaard uses the concept of despair to refer to what it is to not will to be yourself. According to Kierkegaard, to despair is to have a will that never wholeheartedly gathers or unifies itself. The despairing person attempts, out of a kind of reluctance to be themself, to run away from themself. The root of the Danish word for despair used by Kierkegaard, '*fortvivelse*,' is the word '*tvi*', "two," which points towards the fact that the despairing will is spread out in more than one direction.

A person in despair lives with a frustrated will that cannot be gathered together, but runs off in several different directions at once. Kierkegaard gives the concept of despair a special meaning. Traditionally, despair means to be without hope, to have lost hope, which is something very different to having a frustrated or fragmented will. But upon closer examination it makes a lot of sense to describe the condition of a will that cannot gather itself together as hopelessness. So like Kierkegaard, I will use the concept 'despair' to refer to not truly willing.

The famous 20th century theologian Paul Tillich says aptly that for the person in despair, who has lost all hope, there is 'no way out.' Someone who still has a glimmer of hope still has the possibility of seeing or imagining a way out of their predicament. But without hope, one is locked into the situation. Psychologically, this being locked-in is just the sort of condition one finds oneself in when one's will cannot collect itself. For when the will cannot be focussed, but runs off in several different directions at once, one is locked fast in oneself. Instead of getting on with life, one goes around in circles, in an internal war with one's conflicted will. And there's 'no way out' of this war because it takes place on a person's most basic level – that of the will. The war is waged in the person themself, as if their one leg wanted to go to right but the other leg wanted to go left at the same time.

There are some subtle psychological dynamics in play here. For the reason that you, Rasmus, are locked fast in yourself is, as I've said several times, that you look outward and away from yourself the whole time. What at first might look hopeful to you – your constant and not infrequently promising plans for the future – become, on second glance, the cause of your very hopelessness. For your thoughts are of course about a hopeful future. But you always have these thoughts *today*, and in the way in which you have them you're at war with yourself. You want only to have your idea or conception of yourself, but you don't want to have your experience of yourself here and now. You want to think about yourself, but you don't want to *be* yourself. You don't want to be what you are, and what you want isn't what you are. As I've mentioned, your thoughts, plans and worries turn into self-absorption, which makes you never come out of yourself and come into the *now* wholeheartedly. Precisely because you've been taken over by your hope for the future, you become, ironically enough, hopeless in the present.

From a psychological point of view, to have hope or not is therefore less a matter of having a particular future to hope for, than of being able to gather oneself together and come out of oneself. It's this situational hope, this patience in the present moment, which fails for the despairing person, not the hope for something or some plan in particular that will take place in the future. Despair, the condition of hopelessness, is therefore aptly described as a condition in which one has not one, but two wills, which each runs off in its own direction. Kierkegaard also uses the concept 'double-mindedness' about being in despair. The double-minded person both wills and does not will at the same time. They are in two minds – or in seven or fourteen or a hundred minds – and flits around and around on the spot inside themself.

From here on in I'll use the concept 'despair' for not truly willing. So when I try to say in these letters that you must always will to be yourself – that you must be yourself wholeheartedly – this is the same as saying that you must not despair. And at the same time let me say that if there's a central point in everything I write to you, it's this message that you must not despair, that you must will to be yourself. Everything I have written and will write to you flows, as it were, from this centre. For all of this is an attempt to lay out what is contained in this fundamental message, as well as an attempt to describe how you seem to be living in a state of not willing to be yourself.

So if you take anything from my letters, start with this: *don't despair*.

Back tomorrow,
Morten

***

Rasmus,

What right do I have to tell you not to despair? Who decided that you *must* be yourself? What if, quite simply, you just don't want to be yourself? I realise that I'm not speaking to you with any higher authority behind me, and of course it's up to you to decide whether you want to despair or run away from what you are. You're a free man. I'm not your boss. But I can try to describe just what an impossible position you put yourself in when you live in a state of not willing to be yourself. And I can thereby point out how you really have no choice, how you do in fact need to will to be you. But whether you will listen to what I have to say, whether you will do what you should – that's up to you.

When you live in a state of not willing to be yourself here and now, but only will to be yourself in your ideas about the future, you're in conflict with yourself. But because you're blind – or at the very least half-blind – to yourself, you never really pick up on this conflict. If the conflict or contradiction had been of a simple logical character, you would have caught it straight away. If someone said to you that you were both dark-haired and blonde, or that you both were in the supermarket and not in the supermarket, you would have asked for further explanation. But the conflict you're in with yourself doesn't have such a straightforward logical character. It lies within the person itself, and as your person isn't visible to you, it isn't visible to you that there's any conflict at all either. But the conflict isn't lessened just because you can't see it. It just becomes less manageable, and when you *are* the conflict – or your person or will itself is the conflict – then existence becomes practically impossible for you. In that *you* are the conflict itself, 'you' becomes something blurry and washed out, which exists both here and there at the same time. You become an airy and restless being. You're fighting a war in which you find yourself on both sides of the front lines.

* * *

To be in a constant state of wilful conflict is to be sloppy with oneself. It's bad problem-solving, a poor solution to the task of being oneself. Life brings with it the task that you must be yourself and will to do so. And to refuse to take this task on, or at least try to refuse, is sloppy. It's disorderly. That life comes with this task may sound like something I've already said. But I will try here to elaborate on what is really entailed by life's bringing such a task with it. That is, I'll try to elaborate on the consequences it would have for your self-understanding if you accepted that life comes with such a task.

If you accept that life comes with the task that you must not despair, and if you see with sufficient clarity what this task entails, this will have wide-ranging and crucial consequences for your self-understanding. In my previous letters I spoke of how there is something in you, something about your person, which takes precedence over all the plans and ideas you have for life. There is something in you which binds you, and which you cannot run away from. This message in itself might be threatening and humiliating enough for you, someone who has been accustomed to considering yourself to be your own project. Maybe in some unpleasant way the message leaves you playing catch-up to an existence you thought you had mastered. But when I now say that being you at all involves a task for the will, you actually play catch-up in relation to life in a far more decisive sense than was the case in the previous letters.

If being yourself comes with a task for your will itself, this means that all the time – here and now – you are obligated and challenged. It means that in a fundamental sense, existence speaks and you answer – not, as you like to see things, that you speak and existence obeys. Because up to now you haven't seen the fundamental task of being yourself, it's made sense for you to regard existence as something that arranges itself according to your wishes and plans. You've succeeded in getting the career, the partner, the apartment and the friends you wanted, and that sort of thing is of course to a great extent to your own credit. But when it comes to really being yourself, it's a very different tune.

Being yourself properly is about how you respond to the task of willing to be yourself, and as this is always a matter of the will's here and now, you'll never come out on top. The task is constantly challenging and making demands of *your entire person*. The task concerns all of you, all the time. You can never say that now you've finished with this task, and that now you'll go on to new tasks. When we look ahead in hope and dream of the future, we tend to think of ourselves as we are on the other side of the task. We think that when I grow up, when I become rich, when I become Napoleon, when I end up on a Caribbean beach, then I'll no longer have any tasks to face; instead I'll simply be that abstract third person which the pictures promised. But the task comes along with us, which comes as a disappointment for the person who dreamt that they eventually might get out of having to be themself.

No matter what situation you find yourself in, no matter if it's a situation of worry and failure where you are reluctantly thrown back upon yourself, or a situation of elation and success where you are beside yourself with happiness, it's *you* who must find out what it is to be you in that situation – which is to say that you must will to be yourself in that situation.

Best wishes,
Morten

Dear Rasmus,

Today I'll try to conclude the question of what it is to will properly. Let me get straight into it:

The task of being yourself is unconditional. The task doesn't depend upon whether you want to do it, or whether you view it as advantageous to be yourself. The task stands before you regardless of what you think about it, and for you, who has never done anything *but* impose conditions on existence, it would transform your entire world if you understood that there is something that imposes conditions on *you*. It would change your world decisively if you understood that there's something which you can't get around, but which, regardless of how well or badly you behave, continually makes a demand of you: the demand that you must will to be yourself.

Maybe it sounds like I'm making life a bit too hard, by pointing to an unconditional demand which you'll never get rid of. But if you consider closely how you actually live today, you'll discover that this harsh judgement in fact contains a great reprieve.

Today, you never will to be yourself. You always want to be something else – you're always on your way to something better which you think you should be. There's no peace for you, because you're constantly trying to improve yourself relative to the plans and conceptions you've set for yourself. But the unconditional task that you must will to be yourself contains the message that you're actually *allowed to be* yourself. Your despair today is connected to the unhappy notion, which you believe, that being yourself can only be praiseworthy when your life resembles a certain idea or conception. You're constantly waiting for this idea or conception to become a reality. But if you understand that you actually don't have permission to wait, because you, already, now – right now – must be yourself, then you will also understand that in fact you already have permission to be yourself now.

In the endless task of gathering yourself together and willing to be yourself, there is also the great reprieve that you don't need to wait for permission to be yourself. The message "Don't despair!" therefore also contains a further message: that you don't *need* to despair. But you only get this liberating side of the coin if you are willing, with complete seriousness, to understand and comply with the coin's binding and obligating side. The liberation consists just in the fact that you *must*, and that you seriously understand that you must.

I myself wasn't much younger than you are now when I began to realise the things I'm talking about here. I'd already been a priest for some years, and before that I'd also spoken and written about things that sound like what I'm saying here. But it's one thing to understand, and another thing to understand yourself in what you've understood. The deciding factor for me at that particular time was no doubt a mix of several things – age, experience, knowledge, outward changes in life which I'll have to tell you about some other time, and then also that grain of random chance that makes something suddenly fall into place in the understanding. But in any case I remember that suddenly, with a clarity I'd never known before, I understood that *I* really had to be myself. It wasn't just some 'person' that had a task, which is perhaps how I'd have spoken of it before. It was me. This understanding gave me at once both peace and a new excitement about life. It drew a line under the reservations I might have had about life before, and it got my anxiety about the future under control. The future could now be seen in the light of my great task, and each day could then have trouble enough of its own – as well as joy. This understanding of course did not mean that I've never had insecurity or misgivings ever since. But I remember it as one of the most liberating things that has ever happened to me, and the feeling of being set free comes back to me the moment I truly reflect that I must really be me.

***

It might seem to you that I'm trying to destroy you. In previous letters I said that there's something in you that binds you, and which is more decisive in relation to what it is to be you than the ideas and plans you yourself have come up with. I said that in a certain sense you need to give up your self-conception in order to truly be you. Now I'm saying that being you also entails responding to a task that is greater than you, and which you will never be finished with. So not only do I want to bind you to something which wasn't your idea, I also want to have you answer to something that is greater than you. Is this current letter in reality just another step in a cunning attempt to disempower you? In one sense, yes. But is it also an attempt to destroy you as a person? Not at all. On the contrary, as I've also said before, it's an attempt to get you to shine through, to ring true, visibly and audibly.

It's a peculiar characteristic of us humans that it's only when we un-reservedly and unflinchingly answer to something greater than our-selves that we shine through as ourselves. Up to now you've believed that the more achievements you could build up around yourself, the more stories and successes you could dress yourself in, the more you would also will to be yourself. But you've been covering yourself up. You have wrapped yourself in ornaments, and while you yourself believe you've increased, in fact you've diminished. Your answer to life's tasks has become more and more muffled, and eventually one could start to wonder if there was anyone hidden back there behind the ornaments at all.

Just as Abraham, with an open and willing heart, stepped forward before God and said, "See, here I am!" you too need to step forward in life. Until you do that, you will be nothing more than your disguises and evasions. It's only when you step out of the disguises and show yourself, that you really and clearly become yourself. So when I say that to be yourself is to respond to a task that is higher than yourself – it's this *you* I want to highlight. I'm not out to hide you away, but to call you forward, and you are only called forward insofar as you willingly and with a pure heart respond to this task.

Don't misunderstand me: the task I would have you respond to is not something abstract. When I speak somewhat loftily of 'the task,' this is just me trying to formulate that even in your most ordinary, everyday life, there is something which is greater than you, and which demands your response. The thing that is greater than you is that at all times you need to be precisely *you*, precisely where you are. Herein lies the task. But what you answer to, when in a given situation you say 'yes, I will', is not 'the task' in any abstract sense, but merely the given situation's concrete contents and demands.

As said, both in cases of failure and uncertainty and in cases of great success, you need to come forward and show yourself as the one who really is and wills to be yourself. But that also applies just as well in all the ordinary matters that life first and foremost consists in. When you sat in the kitchen with Agneta and Alexander on a quiet afternoon, or later in the evening when you went out to get something to eat, it was here that the task was to be found. And the question to you was simple: Do you want to be here? Do you really? Pay attention to yourself and see what a thorough transformation it would be for you if just once you could bring yourself to answer "yes, I want to" – simply and without reservation. It's in the simple and concrete that you either show yourself or do not show yourself. It's here that Agneta – and the rest of us too – either see someone who clearly and unflinchingly steps forward, or merely see the shadow of someone sneaking off behind the veil of a vanishing act.

✳✳✳

Let me finish today's letter here. I've tried to describe how in my view you 'ought' to be, and what I've said is that you must be yourself, or that you must not despair. In the letters I sent you earlier in the week, I spoke about what 'you' are. But as has become clear in the course of this letter – and as I've probably already mentioned – the character of this 'you' is connected with how you live up to this 'ought.' For it's only when you do what you *ought*, and therefore truly will to be yourself, that *you* – the whole person – stand out clearly. So even being yourself therefore has something to do with the extent to which you are able to understand and respond to the task that you must not despair. Whether you are in fact able to, or will later become able to, respond to this task is another question.

It's possible that you'll never be able to fully and completely will to be yourself; it's possible that you will always live in a greater or lesser degree of despair. It's entirely possible, and it wouldn't be unusual. But that doesn't alter the fact that the fundamental task of not despairing applies to you at all times. The task will continue to exist – regardless of how well or badly you are able to respond to it.

Warm regards,
Morten

FORMS OF NON-DESPAIR

Rasmus,

I skipped a day in our exchange. I hope you weren't waiting on me. I started to write yesterday, but I wasn't entirely sure what I should include in this and the following letters. I also had to go to a hospital appointment in the middle of the day. Nothing serious; just old age.

But it took a few hours away from writing, and I ended up last night deciding that I should wait a little to send you something. But here's a letter for you – if a bit shorter than usual; the rest will follow in the next few days.

* * *

In my last letter, I wrote: Don't despair. But what, you may well ask, does non-despair look like? What is it to *not be* in despair? What's it like to be yourself when you don't despair? What does it feel like? I'll try to answer questions like this in my next letters.

I said that to not despair is to want to be yourself, and so I have of course already said something about what you're like when you don't despair: you will to be yourself. But while this definition is true enough, it's also a little too general and formal to throw much light on the matter. The problem with this definition is that while it's good enough formally, the situations in which you really are and will to be yourself come in countless shades, colours and variations, and with lived content that will often be experienced as something completely different than 'willing to be yourself.' You will to be yourself fully and completely when you are fully and completely engaged in life. And this engagement can appear in countless different ways. If you're just too busy to be yourself – if you're *explicitly* preoccupied with the thought that you must be yourself – that's actually a sure sign that you don't really want to be yourself. On the other hand, you earnestly will to be yourself in those situations in which you are outside of yourself, and move forward in life. And there are innumerable variations of situations like that. The will that is here being shown comes in an endless range of nuances, and your experience of being yourself also comes in an endless range of nuances.

So when I ask what it feels like when you will to be yourself, the description quickly goes awry. For you feel all sorts of different ways. There isn't one particular mood or one particular emotion that describes it better than others. The essence of non-despair has no specific psychological form. The rather general and formal definition "to will to be yourself" therefore has the distinct advantage that it doesn't limit non-despair to a particular mood or emotion. Nonetheless, there are certain psychological phenomena and conditions which suggest more than others that one wants, in a deeper sense, to be oneself. Some ways in which non-despair manifests are more exemplary than others. And so in order to guide you from the general and formal to the more concrete, I'll try to describe five of these: joy, courage, grief, humility, and humour.

Over the next five days, I hope to send you one letter each day on these phenomena. But you'll have to wait until tomorrow for the first letter.

Warmest regards,
Morten

Joy

Joy is one of the clearest expressions of non-despair. Kierkegaard describes joy as being contemporary with yourself, or being present to yourself. This description is apt, because in joy you are purely and totally given over to life – as yourself. Joy is when you step out into the street on a simple and welcome errand; it's when you breathe freely and easily and nourish an unconditional certainty that nothing could be better and nothing more right than doing just this errand this day.

Joy is the opposite of worry. When you are worried, you are non-contemporary with yourself. In worry you're spread out across your worried thoughts about yourself. These thoughts show quite clearly that you are busily preoccupied with yourself – indeed I've also previously described your worry as self-absorption. But you are neither contemporary nor present, because you're either behind or ahead of yourself in your worried thoughts. In joy, by contrast, there is a surrender to life, here and now, in which being yourself isn't a problem, but comes completely naturally.

The claim that you lack joy in your life has run like a red thread through my letters. Your secret and watchful eye, your endless comparison with others, your endless worry and planning for the future brings you into a constant state of unrest that never lets you just find joy in today itself. For you, joy – if such a concept exists in your world at all – becomes something that must come about in the future. But that's the same as saying that joy never happens for you. For the person who isn't happy *now* is never happy.

In a sense, my attempt to describe your condition has been an attempt to help you see how joy is absent from your life, and to then help you see how you can find joy in life. My letters could thus seem to offer a kind of psychological self-help process, at the end of which, if all goes well, you'll find joy. But to read my letters in that way would be a mistake. For joy isn't something that comes at the end. *Joy is either there from the start, or it's not there at all.* When I've said that you lack joy in your life, I haven't then added in any simple sense "because a, b, and c." I haven't pointed out a set of obstacles you need to get out of the way in order to be happy. All I've done is try, through a range of variations, to describe what it really is to be you, an unhappy person. Maybe these descriptions can help you sharpen your attention to yourself and thereby lead yourself onto the right path – that's what I hope. But don't try to use these descriptions as a recipe or user's manual for joy. They aren't suitable for that.

I've talked about how you become yourself best when, in a sense, you destroy yourself, and come out of yourself saying 'yes, please' to life. In joy, this 'yes, please' is unconditional and unlimited. But once again, don't misunderstand me: I'm not saying that if you force yourself to say 'yes, please,' then you'll also become happy. I'm saying that in itself, joy is already there in this 'yes, please.' For when you rejoice completely in life, you've *already* said 'yes, please' to this life. In joy you are willing to just be yourself in just this given situation – for being you here presents no problem, nor is it particularly burdensome. It's part of the essence of joy that when you are joyful, you also will to be yourself, with everything that entails. Joy can be quiet or forceful, it has its own vast register of colours and nuances, but regardless of which colour you find it in – in joy you have already completely said 'yes' to life.

As it is a task for you to will to be yourself, and as joy is a thorough-going form of willing to be yourself, it could also be said that you actually have the task of taking joy in life. Now, I realise that we normally speak of joy as something that happens to us. We talk about joy as something we 'have' or 'experience' on special occasions. Your own concept of joy is probably just like this too: you become happy when something particularly good happens to you. So it might seem perverse to speak of joy as a task. But this contradiction is quite profound, and underlines just how delicate and vulnerable a task it really is. For you can't strenuously and urgently force yourself into joy, but you can try to allow yourself to be happy. You can try to make room for joy. Joy has the exquisite property that in joy, you are outside yourself, but that also means there are limits to how much you yourself can do in the face of joy. If you strain to control it or make it serve you, you remain inside yourself and thereby actually keep joy away. When I say that you *should* be happy, I'm therefore talking about a task which you can't simply carry out without further ado. You can desire joy, and hope for it, but joy has a mind of its own and won't let itself be pressured or stressed. So wait for it, allow yourself to be happy, and be happy when you are happy.

At the same time, beware of false forms of joy. Joy has the double-edged character that its false forms only drive us even further into despair and hopelessness. And the false forms arise the moment you try to make yourself master over joy. If you try to make joy into a part of your self-projects, it will take its revenge on you. For the joy you can define and determine yourself is merely a mask. One who chases a mask of joy will perhaps look happy in an external sense, but in an inward sense will be unfree, coerced and unhappy. Every attempt to cultivate happiness, or straightforwardly turn it into a criterion of success in life, always ends joylessly. There's a risk of turning joy into just such an unhappy project – not least for ambitious and success-hungry souls like you. There is a danger that you'll begin to cultivate joy as a sort of pleasing annexe to the building you're already in the process of constructing. Thus you will be able to orchestrate joy, career, family and friends in what today is regarded as 'a happy life.' But beware: you can very well live this sort of happy life, but in a deeper sense you'll end up doing so joylessly.

Joyful greetings,
Morten

Courage

Like joy, courage contains a fundamental willingness to be yourself. The courageous person goes into life fearlessly and full of confidence. For the brave, there is no hesitation or self-absorbed reservation, but sheer life-momentum.

When one looks at the life you lead, it might initially look as if you live with great courage. You rush into new projects, each more ambitious than the last, and you have the persistence to carry your projects through. But what you display is not courage in the sense in which I'm here using the word. You're ambitious and canny, and at times you even show a degree of willingness to take risks – but that's not the same thing as courage. You only move forward when you've calculated seven, ten or a hundred moves ahead, and when you finally get going, you do so warily and watchfully in fear that your calculations might be wrong. The courage I'm talking about, the courage that appears in a person as a fearless confidence in life, only appears weakly, if at all, in such a fearful and worried existence as yours.

The state of courage contains a thorough trust in life; by contrast, lack of courage contains a thorough mistrust of life. Without courage, you hesitate every step you take. You never dare to set foot on the ground properly, because you're afraid of the ground you walk on. Trembling, you try to put your feet down such that they don't end up touching the ground. And when you can't step onto the ground without actually touching it, you at least try to put your feet down so softly and uncertainly that it only leaves the faintest footprint. Courage, by contrast, presses forward with its full weight. Courage goes into life boots and all – carefree and direct. For courage wants to take part in life.

The trust in life that we're talking about here isn't confidence in specific things or persons. Nor is it trust that specific plans or projects are sure to succeed. It's a deeper form of trust which is inherent in the person, and which the person has with them no matter who or what they meet along the way. While the confidence of courage isn't trust in specific things, it's also important to understand that the confidence of courage isn't a special form of self-confidence, either. I'm not endorsing self-confidence, but confidence itself. It's a peculiarity of our age that people think a deeper confidence or courage in life must be a matter of self-confidence – or self-esteem as it's also known.

That's a ludicrous thought.

Your mistrust of life, your lack of courage, is precisely an expression of your being *too* absorbed in yourself. You're constantly weighing life against your own self-conceptions, and it's clear that the *self*-confidence you are able to show today merely reflects your current evaluation of yourself. Am I any good, or not? Can I have confidence in myself, or can't I? Your task and challenge is just to get out of this constant weighing of yourself and go forward – in confidence.

In Christianity, the trust in life that inheres in the fundamental courage I'm talking about here is traditionally associated with faith. In my letters I've omitted talking about faith, and I'll also keep it short here, for I know that you find it hard to see any deeper meaning in this concept. But let me just say that when Luther, for instance, struggled with his faith in his youth, when he doubted, his lack of faith lay in his lack of *trust* in God. The question wasn't whether God existed – that was simply assumed. For Luther, to win faith was to win trust or confidence that God was good and gracious. And even though God doesn't seem to have the same place in your universe, in human terms you have the same problem as Luther. You don't have trust or confidence in life.

While you and Luther have the same problem in a certain sense, you nonetheless seek different solutions to that problem. The solution of faith that Luther sought is hardly a solution for you, and of course that's fine. But the solutions you try for yourself are, however, hopeless in a far more basic sense. You seem to think that the solution to your lack of courage and your lack of trust in life is to eliminate life's uncertainties. As I've said many times, you seem to be fighting your insecurity by trying to control life and make life fit your own conceptions and narratives. But you're on an endless downward spiral. For the only appropriate answer to insecurity is – security. The only solution to a lack of trust is trust itself. The only solution to a lack of courage is courage itself.

Whatever you might think about Christianity, it has at least never been confused on this point. The Christianity I know has never tried to solve the problems of faith and trust with easy security and cheap guarantees. Again and again it's been repeated to the Christian: only faith can overcome a lack of faith.

Only trust can overcome a lack of trust. So however you stand with your faith and your waning courage, at least learn this little bit of psychology from Christianity: you mustn't seek courage and trust in simple security. You won't find it there. Instead, show courage and trust as best you can in the midst of life's insecurity – that's the only courage and the only trust that counts.

Best,
Morten

Grief

As I said, non-despair has no particular mood or particular emotion. Non-despair isn't necessarily connected to what we regard as positive states. Complete willingness to be what you are needn't be followed by the feeling that one is *happy* to be oneself. In a paradoxical sense, willingness can also be found in the greatest pain. It can be found when being yourself has become absolutely unbearable. I'm not thinking here of those little discomforts or uncertainties which we hurry to get away from. I'm thinking of experiences where one is thrown back upon oneself with such force that the thought of escape becomes futile.

Grief is one such experience.

In grief you no longer want to run away from yourself, because there's no longer anything to run away *to*. In grief's loss, the future and the future's promise of escape are no longer there. While one suffers under the pain of loss, one also knows that no future could relieve this pain. For the future will always be a future without the person we've lost. When the world seems to shut down and loss makes all orientation seem meaningless, it's the future's possibilities with the other person that disappear. The relief we once found in the thought that tomorrow we will realise the hopes we had for a common future is no longer available. Instead of being spread out into the future, we find ourselves gathered together here and now, left behind with our loss.

I mentioned earlier how I myself was called back to reality when Lene died. The same thing happened again when Kathrine died. But Lene's case hit everything with a force all its own. That was probably because she was my daughter, and she was still young. But it's also because of the circumstances of her death. It was both unexpected and long-expected. We knew that it could happen. But when it did happen, it happened suddenly, out of the blue, with no clear reason or warning. The hopes we had for her, and which had sustained us, were suddenly dashed. The possibility of anything ever being good again was gone. The possibility that someday it might turn out that we hadn't failed after all was gone.

I won't try to spell out the horrors I went through. But it felt, literally, as if I'd had a vital organ removed. Up until then I'd lived and breathed in something – a hope, a future – which no longer existed. I couldn't breathe. I couldn't see or hear. I couldn't eat. It happened at the end of a period in which I'd long been preoccupied with my own hopes for my career, and my relationship with Lene had to an increasing degree been based on hope for the future rather than joy in our present life together. Her life was always hard.

There was always fragility, sensitivity and conflict around her. It had always been that way, and as parents that sort of thing certainly didn't make us love her less. But when I consider myself in the time leading up to her death, I think that her condition combined with my own busyness – or self-absorption if you like – had made me impatient. It was as if I'd given up, and put my hope and trust in the thought that what never seemed to succeed in the present would succeed someday, in a better and more problem-free future.

Her death called me back from my dreams and back down to earth with a loss that no longer had any mitigation ahead of it. It took a long time before I even dared to grieve, though. At first I tried to avoid what had happened, tried to avoid understanding that it had happened, and my state was more one of panic than grief. So even though I say that grief hits us with a force all its own and gathers us here and now, there nonetheless also comes a point in grief where the question of courage arises. Do we even dare to grieve? Do we dare to bear at the same time the thought of the person we've lost and the thought that we must now live without her? Or do we try to forget her, or forget her absence?

Only little by little did the courage to both remember and miss Lene sink in. While the feeling of being overwhelmed went away, the grief, the real grief, took its place. That grief has since gone through many phases and transformations. But while it has perhaps become increasingly calm, increasingly clear, it's never diminished. It lives its own inescapable life, and wrong as it might sound, I actually often feel closer to Lene in memory than I managed while she was still alive. I wish it was otherwise. I wish I'd made things better back then. But there was always too much hope, too much disappointment, too much frustration between us for us to ever really feel close. It's different now.

She would have turned forty-five next week as it happens. I'll finish my discussion of grief here. In fact, at first I didn't really intend to talk about grief, let alone about my own grief. I didn't think this theme really belonged in these letters. But I was afraid that my talk of joy and courage was about to sell you on some simple sort of "religion of happiness". As I said, thoroughly willing to be yourself does not have more to do with good moods than bad. It's a matter of being completely willing in the given situation – regardless of what the situation might involve. And so we can discern forms of non-despair in grief just as well as in joy and courage, and so I decided to discuss grief as one of the forms of non-despair.

Warmest regards,
Morten

Humility

The complete willingness in a person that shows itself in various ways in joy, courage, and grief, requires humility. It's in humility that you preserve the understanding that it's you who answers to life, and not life that answers to you.

I described how you always seem to be in the process of covering yourself up and hiding behind your projects and narratives about yourself, whereas being yourself properly is about coming out of your self-conceptions with a pure heart and saying: "here I am." When you cover yourself up and hide yourself, you try to outrun life. You try to put yourself in a situation where you have power, and make life dance according to your tune. And even though at first glance this power might appear seductive, and makes you feel that you are on the way up, it makes you vanish. Only when you come out of yourself and wholeheartedly say 'yes, I will' to the life that has been given to you, do you seriously show yourself. Joy and courage – and in its own way, grief – are complete forms of this wholehearted 'yes.' That's why these feelings are only possible for those who don't see themselves as being beyond or above life, but instead understand themselves as responsible *to* life. Joy and courage are, in other words, only possible for those who remain humble.

That you must *remain* humble doesn't just mean that the task of humility never stops, but also that it knows no limits. For just insofar as it's a constant task to be humble, it also becomes a constant task to relate humbly to the task of being humble. There's no way out of this task. The moment you smugly sit back and think that you've been as humble as you ought to be, and now you deserve a break – or even praise or reward – you're no longer humble. Being humble is a task in which you're always running behind. Always. The moment you think you're in front, you begin to un-humbly shut yourself up inside yourself. Your humility is not something you can adorn yourself with, or something you can be proud of. To be proud of your humility is absurd. Humility is never going to serve you, for it's what sets *you* the task – to be humble – and you're only humble when you humbly answer to this task.

I remember you and I once discussed the question of a person's 'justification' in Christianity. The discussion took place some years ago, and I don't remember specifically what led to it, other than that I'd tried to explain to you that in Protestantism we don't believe that a person can improve themselves by their own efforts and make themselves worthy of God's grace – or justify themselves before God by their own efforts, as it's known. All power belongs to God, whereas a person can do nothing, but must believe in and hope for God's grace. You said that you didn't want a God like that. You said it struck you as unreasonable that God could demand that a person must improve if the person does so by their own hand and without God's help. This discussion took place in a different context, but it has some crucial points of similarity with what I'm trying to say here about humility.

What shone through in that discussion was that you don't like being faced with anything that in a radical sense is greater than yourself. You won't hear of anything in relation to which you're always in the wrong. If you were to have a God, it would be a God that owed *you* something, not the other way around. You want to have a chance to be right in front of this God. You consider it a human right to be able to improve and perfect yourself in order to become admired. That's why you're repulsed by the thought that God isn't also impressed by your good works.

I imagine it's also like that now that I'm talking to you about humility. You will probably want to hear about the task of humility, but in fact you will only want to hear about it if I can also tell you how to complete this task and get something out of it. But I certainly can't do that, for the point is just that you must be humble.

I realise that our views of life conflict here. But however dissatisfying it must be for you to hear that there's something – in Christianity or in life as a whole – that's greater than you, and which you can't have power over, I still wish you'd look up and see the infinite power and liberation to be found in discovering your own limits. The prison you've locked yourself in is indeed a prison created from your own unstoppable notions of self-improvement. If you never encounter a boundary that says *thus far and no further*, your self-improvement can continue indefinitely.

Humility, or the task of humility, is just such a boundary. Humility isn't impressed or seduced by the fact you're a fantastically successful person. You'll never entice it over to your side. It simply stands there with its task and says: be humble. Perhaps it's a big task that humility sets, but precisely because the task is so big, at the same time it sets you free from yourself.

Humbly,
Morten

Humour

While humility is a precondition for being thoroughly willing, to maintain that thoroughness takes humour. It's humour that prevents thoroughness from ossifying and turning into its opposite. Of the phenomena I've mentioned in these letters – joy, courage, grief, humility and humour – humour is in fact the most complex. While joy, courage, grief and humility all express a certain straightforward and complete purity or wholeheartedness, there's something double-edged or contradictory about humour. Humour isn't pure in itself, but is what bends and relativises purity – precisely in order to preserve it.

The fact is that every time someone wholeheartedly takes hold of themself and strikes out boldly into the world, as I have been urging you to do, they are also on the way to shutting themself in and becoming half-hearted. Wholeheartedness never exists in a pure form. Or to put it differently: one is never simply good. For as soon as you positively say 'yes' to being yourself in a given situation, you are already in the process of negatively getting stuck in that situational conception of yourself and locking yourself into it. So when I say that you, today, are locked inside your self-conception, that is not a state you will ever be able to overcome entirely. You will always need to orient yourself in life with specific ideas or notions about yourself, and you will always be on the way to locking yourself in with them.

That you orient yourself according to specific ideas or representations is of course perfectly in order – that's life – but as soon as you do so, those notions and ideas set out to trap you. What should have been a wholehearted, open boldness is on its way to becoming a simplistic and one-sided insistence on a particular idea. The unconditional will to be yourself is, in other words, always on the road to becoming a conditioned will, one that only wills in relation to specific conceptions, ideas or projects.

Even this very talk of wholeheartedness is also, all the time, on course to become a one-sided hectoring about a particular idea of wholeheartedness. If you do not have humour, wholeheartedness becomes a ridiculous little project in which, in zealous pursuit of that whole, full and pure heart, you stand and shout "all or nothing!" like Ibsen's Brand - while you shut yourself up more and more inside the idea of wholeheartedness. As a higher form of humility, humour is that elasticity or flexibility in a person that allows them to keep the sense that, regardless of which way they choose, the path will be full of limitations.

In humour, they preserve their understanding that they must not think themself already safe and sound just because this path has been chosen. In this way, humour is a diversion and indulgence which, in a sense, reduces wholeheartedness, not in order to make it luke-warm and half-hearted, but rather to let it live on, struggling and striving, aware of its own limits and fallibility.

St. Paul writes to the Romans that nothing is impure in itself. But the opposite is also true: nothing is pure in itself either. Perhaps we have pure ideas about purity, but for living human beings, everything also contains its opposite. To put it in philosophical language, everything is dialectical. The pure heart is an ideal, which always appears in a tainted form because, as I've said, it is always in the process of locking itself in even as it opens itself. And humour understands this duality. Humour walks on two feet, as it were. If you've ever noticed how easy it is to catch a humourless person on the wrong foot, the explanation is quite simple: they only stands on one foot. Someone who lives without humour does not see the duality in their own situation, but thinks they can simply and straightaway be good. They speaks in sim-plistic, literal terms and thinks that because they *say* 'wholehearted,' they can also *be* wholehearted without any difficulty.

Someone without humour has not understood that they themself are something other than their own idea or conception. That makes them, at best, naïve; but more often it makes them annoying, and not in-frequently it makes them dangerous. Insofar as they don't see that the opposite of their idea also dwells within them, they stands smugly on that one foot of theirs, suspecting no danger, until humour or irony – humour's strict little sister – comes by one day and pokes them. So they fall head over heels, for they know of nothing to hold onto except their idea, and lose their balance just when they are no longer permitted to believe that they are identical with their idea.

To poke a humourless person is like tipping a sleeping cow. They were both standing there just fine – stiff, rigid and self-satisfied – and suddenly they are lying on the ground kicking and flailing, wondering what on earth just happened.

Sorry if I got a little carried away there, having fun at the expense of humourless people. The art, naturally, is not to see and expose other people's lack of humour, but to see how, all the time, you yourself are falling into feeling too secure in your one-sidedness. And for the record, let me also mention that if nothing is good in itself, that goes for humour as well. Humour's diversion and indulgence can make one blasé and apathetic. Even humour itself needs to be kept on the leash of humour's own duality, so to speak. Take care not to turn humour into a weapon that then turns itself against you.

And with that humourless admonition, let me close this letter, and my attempt to describe the forms of non-despair. I hope that at least some of the descriptions have made sense to you. My next letters will be of quite a different character than the last few, but more on that later – in my next letter.

**

You won't be hearing from me for the next week or so. As I said, on Monday I'll be heading to Berlin and visiting Margrethe and the family, and I won't have a chance to write while I'm down there. I'm looking forward to seeing them. Since they've moved there we don't get to visit each other as often as we should. I haven't booked a flight yet.

I'm thinking of driving if the weather isn't too bad. A little road trip might be fun. But don't say anything to your mother or Margrethe. They just think I'll crash or pass out or whatever. They needn't know until it's strictly necessary. Also, what does one do with kids in Berlin these days? The zoo? Again? Margrethe has taken the whole week off, and Frederik is off school, so no doubt we have a full program ahead of us. Thomas doesn't have time off though. He probably even has to go away for a couple of days mid-week. I'm looking forward to the next few days. I hope your days at home with Alexander will also be good; I'm sure they will be. Take care, and talk soon.

Best,
Morten, shortly in Berlin.

LIFE ON EARTH

Rasmus,

I heard a rumour that your mother had coffee with Klaus while I was away. She didn't say anything about it. Is there anything to this rumour? Know anything about it? Espresso or latte grande? I should probably have spoken to her. Hmmm, maybe I should try to reign in my curiosity for a while instead. I know I already said it several times yesterday, but it was really encouraging to hear that your days with Alexander went so well. You've made great progress in a really short period of time. It probably won't be long until you've got your old strength back again. That's really lovely to see. Just great. But you must still take care not to push yourself too hard. As I said, the road trip gave me a rich opportunity to think about my next letters, and it has gradually become fairly clear what I would like to say. I'll jump into it tomorrow.

Morten

Dear Rasmus,

As I've mentioned, this letter will be of a somewhat different character to the last few letters I've sent you. Those letters were about you, and what it is to be you. This letter is still about you, but with a different focus. The 'you' I've been talking about up to now is a 'you' that belongs to a particular world and a particular view of life. When I've been able to think about what it really is to be you – and so also about how you ought to be – this 'ought,' in other words, is connected to a larger conception of life. In what follows, I'll try to describe this larger conception of life. Admittedly, such a description can only be piecemeal, tentative and incomplete – even if I write thousands of pages on the topic. But the fact that my powers of authorship are limited just makes your task as a reader all the greater. It's my hope that you'll try to mobilise so much imagination and flexibility of thought that even my piecemeal descriptions may give you a fuller and more accomplished understanding of the topic.

In a previous letter I wrote that I wanted to return to discussing what I understand by "the ordinary life." I'd like to continue this discussion here. But I won't do so under the heading "the ordinary life," but under a heading which is more fitting given the points I'll try to make: "life on earth." This letter is an attempt to describe the conception of life that this concept "life on earth" contains. I've written about how being you demands that you really *will* in a complete way to be yourself – that is, how you need to will to be your entire person, with all the happy and unhappy characteristics and circumstances that involves. In this letter I'll try to set out how the idea I'm calling "life on earth," and the fact that you must be precisely you and nobody else, are two sides of the same coin.

They're two sides of the same coin because the idea that you must will to be the concrete person you are is connected to a more comprehensive conception of what it is to live properly. It's this conception of the 'proper life' which I'm calling life on earth. If you develop an understanding of what this conception entails, you'll be better able to understand my motivation for criticising your current way of life. You'll be able to better understand how the self you cultivate must of necessity come to grief in life – that is to say, in life on earth. It should thereby also become clearer to you which direction I'd like to see you move in; and maybe you'll even catch a glimpse of the riches contained in the life on earth I'm talking about.

The idea or conception of life on earth expresses something distinctive about our culture or history. Others have tried to describe what I call life on earth as, for example, "everyday life" or "workaday life." These various descriptions all have something going for them, for life on earth is indeed concerned with the most everyday and ordinary things in life as we know it. But instead of 'everyday life' or 'workaday life,' I'm choosing the more open concept 'life on earth' in order to avoid limiting the discussion to excessively well-defined conceptions of what such a life must contain. Perhaps my concept will sound a little too pompous or sentimental. But bear with me. The concept is provisional, and merely implies or suggests a semantic direction. If it only succeeds in doing that reasonably well, I'll be more than satisfied.

***

Life on earth is a Christian idea. And to a large degree it's a Protestant idea. Or rather, the idea of life on earth became possible through Christianity and is given particular emphasis in Protestantism. This idea has played a decisive role in the development of the culture you were born into and grew up in. In other words, it's something you take part in, regardless of whether or not you profess to be Christian. For while Christianity may have receded into the background, it seems clear that the idea of life on earth remains the focal point for the life we live today.

Life on earth isn't an idea or conception which can be defined just like that. It's too extensive for that. Yet we live right in the midst of this idea, and it's the idea that describes and defines us rather than we who describe and define the idea. But if you pay attention to the fundamental facts that have allowed this idea to come into being, it's possible that this attention will provide the little nudge that will help you to notice other things, which in turn will help you notice still other things, and so on until the idea of life on earth ever so quietly begins to fall into place for you.

There are two fundamental Christian-Protestant factors which set the idea of life on earth in motion. If you understand these fundamental factors with sufficient gravity, you'll be in a position to start seeing for yourself just how distinctive and extensive a matter life on earth is for those of us who live this life. These two fundamental factors go together and can't be considered without each other. Try to think about one without the other and it all goes wrong – both in life and in thought. The fundamental factors are that:

1) The person you are, in precisely the life you've been given, with all the sorrows and joys this life entails, is infinitely valuable. For it is an expression of God's will that you are just this person and live just this life.

2) Our distance from God is infinite. We have no possibility of 'raising ourselves up' above life and creating or shaping our selves before God. We can and must do nothing other than live as who we are, where we are.

The first fundamental factor contains a radical and unconditional positive evaluation of the individual person's worth and value. Precisely as the person they are, in precisely the life they live, right here and now, the person is infinitely valuable. At the same time the other fundamental factor contains a radical and unconditional denial that a person must try to make themself more than or other than they are – for a person can't make themself into something of more worth or value than what has already been bestowed by God in any case. This duality expresses two sides of the same coin; and if they only have one side, a person becomes insufferably self-aggrandising and self-worshipping – because they have suddenly become ever so worthy – and if they only have the other side, then all imaginable forms of inhumanity and oppression are given free reign. It's in this delicate tension between human life as infinitely valuable and human life as infinitely subordinate to God that life on earth takes place.

It was Luther who saw most clearly that life in this tension was what Christianity had been trying to teach us the whole time. He therefore said that, first, life must be lived in joy for everything as it is – that if God has a plan for us, then it must be that we should live in joy, gratitude and trust in God just as we've been created. And secondly, he said that we should stop believing that we could become closer to God through practicing churchly magic or good works. He rejected every notion that we could make ourselves more distinguished or righteous before God than we already were – God was too great for that. After having said this, Luther left the monastery, married and continued his work as a priest outside the monastic walls.

There's a certain joyful embracing of life in all of this, but an embrace that at the same time is a very serious business, because the embrace and the joy are now a task that God sets for us in this life. And so life on earth, the everyday life of both drudgery and celebration that we already take part in, becomes infinitely valuable. Now nothing but this life matters anymore. And conversely, suddenly *everything* matters, every single detail of life. Every single piece of the everyday and the life we have here with each other acquires its worth because the task now lies precisely here.

Luther abandons every attempt to make the task simple and limited. It doesn't help to go into the monastery, it doesn't help to follow the priests' prescriptions for good works, it doesn't help to buy one's salvation from the church. Nothing helps. Or rather: everything helps. For everything has now become important, and someone who doesn't will to live life in its multiplicity, who believes they can escape by choosing a 'smarter way,' such as what the church or the priest or whoever else prescribes, is cheating. Everything helps, everything is important, but nothing is certain.

Because life in its entirety is now given the place it should have, and because God can no longer be placated with special religious tricks, nothing is secure once and for all. Life is uncertain, and big, bigger than you – but it's just this life that you must live. You mustn't whine or beg for shortcuts to 'something better' or more secure, but live in joy, right now. It's here that the entrance to what I'm calling life on earth is to be found.

When in the previous letters I've tried to describe how extensive a task it is to be yourself, and how you need to will this task – for good or ill and with all the uncertainty which this entails – this is related to the infinitely high value Protestant Christianity places upon this life. The fact that you have no higher purpose than simply being you, and the fact that being you is serious business, are connected by this Protestant history. And when I've spoken of how it's really your *will* that is the difficulty, again this is connected to the fact that when the life you've been given is infinitely important, then you must will everything.

You mustn't just carry out a few select works, but must be willing to do *all* life's works – willing to do them completely, which is to say with courage, joy, and humility.

I'll continue this tomorrow.
Morten

* * *

Rasmus,

I'll pick up where I left off: I want to argue that if this radical positive evaluation of the already-given life hadn't taken place, and if this evaluation wasn't divinely sanctioned, then we would have had a world where life on earth would never have had inviolable worth in itself. Instead, the value of life could only be thought of in terms of prevailing human or cultural standards. That is, the value of life would only be relative and would only be measured by the success one could achieve in the dominant cultural system, and so in comparison to other people.

If it isn't stressed with infinite emphasis that being exactly who you are, where you are, is the finest and greatest task, the door is opened for a flood of comparisons, conflicts, suspicions and dissatisfactions. And this flood is an uncontrollable torrent that can never stop itself, but can only increase. There's no bulwark to hold the flood back. If this happens, people will be constantly busy, not with living their lives, but with making something of themselves – comparatively.

Just look at the pre-Christian cultures closest to ours. The Greeks had no higher concept of life than its endless perfecting within the existing order. Life in Ancient Greece was a contest of wisdom, virtue, and beauty. Attractive ideals, maybe, but a contest nonetheless, and life had no value over and above that contest, no absolute human worth. In addition, only a small, dominant minority of free citizens could take part in this contest at all. The idea of life's inviolable and infinite worth, regardless of the individual person's public status, was nowhere to be found. And the Icelanders, whose sagas are arguably our closest source for understanding how life might have been here in Scandinavia if Christianity hadn't taken hold, show the same traits. Here and there in the sagas we can indeed see a rugged, individual sense of humour emerge and so, perhaps, a hint of a certain bold humanity in the Norse warrior-culture. But on the whole, the Icelanders behave like apes on horseback. They beat each other with clubs and beer-mugs and can't imagine any greater bliss than conquering the island's largest farm. With the Greeks and the Icelanders you don't find any positive evaluation of the ordinary, everyday, laborious life in itself. Life on earth hadn't yet found its own unconditional worth.

If you begin to understand how special it is that you actually live in a culture that values life on earth, your anxiety over 'not being anything special' or 'just being ordinary' will dissipate. You'll understand that the ordinary isn't even that ordinary after all, but is the expression of a very special historical circumstance. If you develop intellectual maturity to such a degree that you seriously understand that everything – everything! – might have been different, the ordinary will no longer seem quite so ordinary. It's only to childish, or at best adolescent, souls that the ordinary is *merely* ordinary.

Every time I try to think through what we in our culture deem to be ordinary, I'm struck by greater and greater wonder at the rich idea of the life that lies beneath the seemingly familiar surface of the ordinary. I think the same will happen for you if you begin to see the complex ground of everyday life.

***

I don't write these things because I find it interesting in itself to lead you to complex historical realisations. I write it because I can't help but notice how you seem to suffer under your concepts of life. The irony is that while you're conditioned by the Christian idea of life on earth, you try to solve life's problems for yourself with pagan strategies – strategies that remind me of those competitive Greeks or conquering Icelanders. You don't know that you're conditioned by the Christian idea of life on earth, but it dominates you all along, and in that sense it's the true source of your frustration. By that I mean that you can't help but feel and expect that life, your life in particular, ought to have a special, unconditional worth. And as if that wasn't enough, you can't help being secretly ashamed that you don't experience life as unconditionally valuable. You are ashamed that you can't stand being yourself and need to flee from yourself. In Christian terms: you know well enough that you're sinning when your life isn't lived as infinitely valuable.

You know, even if in an inarticulate and unclear way, that something is wrong when you never come to experience life's unconditional worth. But because it's all so unclear and inchoate – because you have no concept of where all your implicit expectations come from – the problem never develops into anything more than a mute dissatisfaction. On the basis of this frustration you throw yourself into projects of outward conquest, since you assume that if you just conquer enough outwardly, unconditional worth will also begin to appear inwardly. What you never understand is that what you can conquer outwardly only has value within the relative sphere where more always wants more, and where enough is never enough. No absolute or unconditional worth is ever reached here.

While the conquering Icelanders were perhaps a bit simple in their conceptions of life, there's something rather tragicomic hanging over your existence. You want to have unconditional and absolute worth in a relative way. Like a child trying to put a square peg in a round hole, you try to put two things together that can't be put together. That's the comedy. And the less you succeed, the more determinedly and frustratedly you try. That's the tragedy.

But you're not alone in that frustration. You're part of a world that long ago landed on the earth and no longer knows why. Life on earth is everything that we have today, but we have it in a confused way that lacks perspective. God placed us on earth in a radical and total sense, and it was God that started us living precisely this life on earth. But then he took his leave, or we took our leave of him, and what was left was us on earth. We were left with the same expectations which we'd had all along, that this life should be something special, but without being able ourselves to provide life with the energy and seriousness that realising these expectations would require. And so for a long time now we've been floating around, banging into one another like dinghies in a tepid and overcrowded harbour. For a long time we've been unable to connect ourselves to the power that would allow us to set off and get our boats under sail. Life has collapsed around us because the pole that used to hold life up has disappeared.

You can cry over stories of decline like this, or you can wax ironic about them if you have the talent for that sort of thing. But you can also rejoice that we're still in fact here, here on earth. We have not yet been driven off into other conceptions of life, but we struggle, perplexed and stubborn, to get *this* life to work. The pain and confusion that follows from this has something heartbreaking and touching about it, but it also comes with a certain hope. The pain provides its own indirect evidence that in spite of all confusion we set no life higher than this very life on earth. And so there should still be a chance that one day we'll be willing to undertake the laborious job of rediscovering the ideas, values and duties that truly belong to this life. And in the meantime we're probably coping well enough with a certain amount of pain and confusion. Where there's life, there's hope, as they say, and while we're willing to let this life hurt just a little – then there should be plenty of hope.

I'll stop here for today. Hopefully I'll be able to conclude this question of life on earth tomorrow.

Best wishes,
Morten

✳✳✳

Dear Rasmus,

If you're going to find your way back from the special and successful life you dream about today to the ordinary life which in a deeper sense you're part of, you'll need to begin to really see this ordinary life and value it for what it is. Try to focus your attention on life on earth as it unfolds today, and see what deep and complex ideas are expressed in it. It will certainly never become clear and certain to you once and for all what life on earth consists in. It's something we can't know or describe once and for all, because life on earth – our valuing of ordinary, everyday life – is precisely the expression of a fundamental openness which says that no specific or limited life-content in itself can save us. When everything is important, when one must will everything, you can't define anything in particular as the answer to life's problems.

To put things a little more philosophically, it's an infinite task that has no determinate finite solution. At the same time life is lived in history, and its specific contents change over time. But nonetheless, in a certain sense our lives are shaped by this fundamental openness. Traces of that openness can be found in some general features and main tendencies that remain definitive for our conception of life.

Try to look closely. Take a look at life's most ordinary ordinarinesses, and see what hopes, expectations and destinies are tied to them. Look at the people around you and everything they hope for and fear. See how they rejoice when they find each other, and break down when they split up again. See how they fret when their children aren't as talented as they'd hoped. Or when they don't get the job they'd dreamed of. Listen to pop music's plea for happiness. Listen to the studio host's excited cries. Look at the clash between economics and idealism. Look at the flags on the motorway. Behold this diverse mix of struggle and levity. Or better yet, look at you and Agneta. See how you've lived in this ordinariness, and how you – both – have been terrified by the thought that one day you might lose it. See how far you'll now go to repair the damage that must have occurred. Look at the enormous current of strenuous and nervous striving in life on earth and see how you yourself are right in the thick of it.

You must fix your eyes on ordinariness, but not because you should begin to idolise it. You mustn't develop any sort of sentimental joy over things 'that look ordinary' – I don't deal in those sorts of banalities. Rather, you should use the ordinary to relativise the narrow conception of life you now adhere to. It's true of everyone who lives on earth that the openness which has been our task right from the start is always in danger of closing up, and we begin instead to worship or glorify a limited part of life. As God isn't there anymore and no longer holds life on earth in his hands with the injunction to will everything in this very life, there's a constant looming danger that life will begin to narrow or fragment.

As people have strong hopes for their lives with each other, for their children's futures or for their own success, hidden in this hope is a broader hope that all will be well with life on earth as a whole. There's a hidden, comprehensive hope for life in general. Or at least, hopefully there is. For when people are placed on earth without God, there's a constant danger that they'll over-emphasise the pursuit of their individual projects. They find it hard to maintain a wider perspective and become unhealthily dependent upon individual matters – and so they in fact lose hold of life just as they're struggling fiercely for it. When God goes out the front door, idols tumble in through the back door. The person who isn't stopped by something infinitely large quickly falls into worshipping small things as if these small things were infinitely great in themselves. God, being something quite different to life on earth and infinitely superior to life on earth, guaranteed that life on earth never got stuck in itself. Those of you who live without God therefore live in great danger of losing life. It requires your constant attention to life in its entirety in order to not fall into worshipping specific parts of it. So try to constantly hold your life-projects up against the big picture that is life on earth as a whole, and don't let your limited projects and self-conceptions destroy your will to take part in this life in a more comprehensive sense.

For example, when I used to criticise your parents' political projects, that was never because of these projects themselves. I realise it might have looked that way. But my problem with their projects was never actually the things they wanted. It was rather all the things they *didn't* want. They were always a bit fanatical and one-sided in their projects. They always seemed to live off the notion that if the world would just adjust itself according to some particular and limited ideas, then all of life's problems would be overcome. They lacked a sense of the whole, and fell in love with the parts.

Their political fervour has long since cooled, and I don't want to dwell on all that. I mention it because I can't help but notice how one generation's excesses in one direction are replaced by the next generation's excesses in another direction. So long as we live this life on earth more or less without perspective, the price we pay is that we'll end up flittering between excesses in this way. *You* denounced political or collective fanaticism and chose instead a career-driven, individualistic fanaticism. But the fact is that politics and careers can both be fine things. It's fanaticism or excess itself that's dangerous. The problem is the one-sided or exaggerated choice of one of life's elements.

I described humour as that which maintains wholeheartedness and prevents it from hardening. That same humour can be said to be required in life's more outward activities which I'm talking about here.

Fanaticism lacks humour, it can't see its own dark side – precisely because it's one-sided.

If there's one thing your parents and their generation lacked amid all their political projects, it was probably humour. They lacked gentleness and forbearance in relation to the life that went beyond their own projects. So at some point either their projects or life had to give way. And as far as I'm concerned, life outlasted them. Remember humour. And remember too that even your attentiveness to the elements of ordinary life needs humour, because you'll never know with any real certainty precisely what these elements consist in.

Earthly greetings,
Morten

YOU WITHOUT GOD

Dear Rasmus,

My letters to you are nearing their conclusion. In my most recent letters I've moved beyond my message to you – don't despair! – into a discussion of the understanding of life that this message involves. It's best that I stop before I go so far afield in this discussion that my message becomes confused or is forgotten. But on the basis of my last letter there's one question I'd like to take a step further before I finish writing. The question is how you who don't have God stand in relation to this task of being yourself. I'll be pointing out, in a somewhat vague way, a certain danger – and also a certain opportunity – which you who don't believe in God face in relation to this task of being yourself.

In my last letter I described how people who live without God tend to fall into idolatry. As soon as there's no longer something to hold all of life on earth in infinite importance, we each begin to worship our own limited ideas and projects. Without God, we quickly fall into limited conceptions of ourselves, and so also into limited conceptions of our great task in this given life on earth, that each of us individually must will to be ourselves. There's nothing that holds our noses to the grindstone in this great task, and so we'd rather shirk that task in favour of smaller ones. You yourself are an example of the obsession with details and specifics that set in when there's nothing that ties you to yourself. You want to be free of the totality in which you find yourself – and instead want to have definite and limited ideas about yourself which you can oversee and define for yourself.

But who on earth could oblige you to carry out the great task of being yourself? I can try to do so, as someone who knows you and cares about you. But I have no true authority over you. Those of you who live without God recognise no true authority. You can choose to listen to what I'm saying, or you can choose not to. There's nothing that drives you to make one choice over the other. I've tried, as best I could, to show you how your state of not willing to be yourself is impossible, that with your divided half-will, you live in a conflict with yourself, which contradicts the very task of being yourself. Maybe you're able to realise that there really is such a contradiction; maybe you accept my analysis of your condition and task, maybe you really think everything I've said is correct. But even then, there's nothing that drives you with any sort of compelling necessity to will properly. The wholeheartedness I ask for is a matter of the will, and if you won't will – well, then, you won't will, not even if you understand and agree with what I say.

If you'd been a believer, if you'd had God, then it would have been clear to you that your condition is one of rebellion against God. Not willing to be who you are is ingratitude, a defiance of the one who gave you life. Offended, you blame your maker for the fact that you must be you, and instead will to be allowed to make do with your own ideas about yourself. If God had had a place in your world, one might have asked you, in your rebelliousness and indignation, what Paul asks: "But who are you, a human being, to talk back to God? Shall what is formed say to the one who formed it, 'Why did you make me like this?'"

Now, Paul's outburst might leave you unmoved, but the question itself – who are you to talk back to God? – is worth dwelling on for a moment. Paul's question is of course rhetorical, but as a question it's actually quite interesting. For what sort of person would talk back to his God? What can we say about a person who would do this? Obviously he's not too bright. There's also something unintentionally comic about him if he thinks that he's the one who makes demands of God, not the other way around. The sort of person who could be offended and insulted by his God must, in a basic sense, lack a concept of himself. His must be a vague and confused existence. I won't go any deeper into an analysis of this person's psychology and self-understanding, but it's clear on even the most cursory glance that, humanly speaking, his is a troubling case.

Paul's retort, *who are you?* can't be directed at you, Rasmus, because you don't talk back to God. You just don't will to be yourself. But even though in that sense you can't be said to be in rebellion against God – you're not rebelling against anyone at all – there's nonetheless something absurd in your position. Or rather, your position is absurd *because* you aren't rebelling against anyone. If you at least had a God you could berate, you could live in the hope that one day God would have mercy on you and say that you no longer had to be you. A somewhat unserious believer who worships a somewhat unserious God can live quite happily with notions like that. But you, on the other hand, who has no one to blame, no-one to direct your complaints to: who do you rebel against when you don't will to be you? Who do you appeal to? You complain out loud in an empty space as if you've never really understood that no-one out there is listening. And thus it nonetheless ends up being relevant to ask you, like Paul, *who are you, really?* Who are you to talk back to... nothing? Who are you to yell at the sky?

Have you, somewhere along the line, maintained faith in some particular god who will ultimately help you? Do you hope that someday the cards will be dealt anew? If you don't believe in anything other than the given world, then it's crazy not to will this world. You, who are without God, have said 'no' to every idea that there might be something beyond this world. But at the same time, you won't say 'yes' to *this* world. This expresses a confusion that you can only avoid being astonished by if you have spent many years getting used to it. If, over the course of a lifetime, you hadn't become used to this state and come to see it as normal, you, as someone who isn't lacking a sense of logic, might wonder yourself at such an inconsistency.

Without God, there's nothing that holds you to your task of being yourself. But without God, it also becomes all the more clear that not willing to be yourself is pointless. So while you perhaps stand more alone, are more fragile and more easily seduced than the believer whose nose is held to the grindstone by God, there's also a certain opportunity to be found in your situation. You have the opportunity to realise your task with total clarity. If you call to mind what is really entailed by not believing in anything beyond the given, it should be able to become clear to you how every way out of this given is shut, and that there's really nothing else to do except – be yourself.

This clarity is your chance. It's your advantage over the believers. For strictly speaking this clarity is something which very few believers achieve. The believer is perhaps set the task of being themself by God, but faces the problem that – human as they are – they can rarely help hoping that God will come and relieve them of the task. To really take God's task seriously and not to fall into blaming God and begging God to re-do his work – to give one a more pleasant task – is something few, if any, manage. In other words, the believer is always in danger of coming to worship God as an idol. Instead of willingly taking on their task, they fall again and again into harnessing God for their own ideas and projects. As soon as religious seriousness fails them, they try to make God their servant instead of, as they ought to, remaining in God's service.

You don't have this problem. You'll never come to hitch God to your wagon. You start more pure than the believer. Your task is more indisputable right from the outset – because you have no-one to negotiate with. In your case there are absolutely no grounds for hesitation or deliberation on whether you will to be yourself or not. But whether you'll be able to translate this pure start into a life of willingness, I can't say. Whether courage and joy will be able to set in for you, with full effect in this indisputable life, or whether you'd rather continue being scared and seeking shelter in limited ideas and projects, I don't know.

I can point out the opportunity. But whether it can become a reality for you must show itself to the person who actually lives your life – that is, you.

✳ ✳ ✳

I would have liked to have rounded off my writings to you with this letter. But in the course of the letter I seem to have reached such a high pitch that I won't be able to find a suitable exit point to land on. I'll let the letter stand, and come back in the next few days. Have a good evening.

Best wishes,
Morten

CONCLUSION

Dear Rasmus,

This morning I again had a meeting at the Ministry and again ate lunch by the lakes on the way home. The last time I sat there, ice was beginning to cover the water and winter was well underway. The ice is gone now, and the beginnings of spring hang in the air. This must mean that it's been a long time since I started writing to you. I hadn't foreseen such a long process. Things took hold; there was so much I wanted to say. I still have my doubts that I really said all of it.

When I look back at the series of letters, one way or another they all seem to miss the mark. But it could be that you'll nonetheless find something useful in what I said. I hope so. In any case you won't hear from me again for now. I'm looking forward to living a more ordinary life with you again. Even though the things I've tried to say have been very much on my mind, it must be time to stop lecturing you.

I have an appointment at the hospital tomorrow. They wouldn't let me off the hook this time. Before long, maybe I myself will need some of the courage I've been preaching about. In that case, you can be the one who gives me the sermon. We'll see. The rumour about your mother's coffee date has also been confirmed. I finally got to talk to her yesterday. Apparently it wasn't just coffee they drank, and well into the evening. I hope it works out for her. And I hope things work out for you, Rasmus. I hope you'll have wind in your sails again soon. I hope we'll soon see you living at full strength – full of courage, joy, and hope. All best for now, and see you again soon. I'll stop here.

Warm regards,
Morten